PREPARE TO SELL YOUR COMPANY

PREPARE TO SELL YOUR COMPANY

A Guide to Planning and Implementing a Successful Exit

L B BUCKINGHAM

howtobooks

Published by How To Books Ltd,
Spring Hill House, Spring Hill Road,
Begbroke, Oxford OX5 1RX. United Kingdom.
Tel: (01865) 375794. Fax: (01865) 379162.
info@howtobooks.co.uk
www.howtobooks.co.uk

How To Books greatly reduce the carbon footprint of their books by sourcing their
typesetting and printing in the UK.

British Library Cataloguing in Publication Data
A catalogue record for this book is available from the British Library

ISBN 978 1 84528 328 5

Produced for How To Books by Deer Park Productions, Tavistock, Devon
Typeset by PDQ Typesetting, Newcastle-under-Lyme, Staffs.
Printed and bound by Cromwell Press Group, Trowbridge, Wiltshire

NOTE: The material contained in this book is set out in good faith for general guidance
and no liability can be accepted for loss or expense incurred as a result of relying on
particular circumstances or statements made in the book. The laws and regulations are
complex and liable to change, and readers should check the current position with the
relevant authorities before making personal arrangements.

Contents

Acknowledgements

This has been a 'long distance project', which would not have been completed without the support of my family, to whom I send my thanks.

I am grateful also to Ian Ritchie for his encouragement, and common sense.

Ray Harris is credited with persuading me to write this book, and I thank him for his constructive comments throughout the assignment.

Being a 'non-techy' person I must mention and thank Ian Makinson, Oona MacDonald and Claire Mogford for their expertise and help with my computer difficulties.

I am indebted to Cathy Mansell, an inspirational fellow writer, who motivated me to complete this undertaking, and Jean Chapman for her introduction to the ways of the world of publishing.

I must thank also the following, whose works I have consulted in the course of my preparations.

Andrew Heslop *How To Value and Sell Your Business*
Paul S. Sperry and Beatrice H. Mitchell *Selling Your Business*
Gary Morley *How To Sell Your Business and Live Happily Ever After*

I hope that you, the reader, will find this book helpful on your road to exit.

L. B. Buckingham

Introduction

From the earliest days of owning my first business, I realised that the assets and substantial wealth building up within it could be capitalised by actually selling the company. Early recognition of this gave me time to make and implement the relevant decisions and actions that would even further improve the company's attributes, and thus its valuation and sale price.

'Prepare To Sell Your Company' draws on this experience, showing how to develop an exit strategy that will deliver to you:

- a company sale timed to suit your best interests;
- the maximum in tax-efficient sales receipts;
- a company demonstrating obvious future potential, thereby ostensibly increased value;
- a company attractive to a wide range of eager potential purchasers.

'Prepare To Sell Your Company' also shows you:

- how to calculate the value of your business;
- how to recognise what buyers want;
- how to groom the company to get the best price from its sale;
- the sale process from beginning to end, highlighting pitfalls to avoid and precautions to take;
- how to deal with the Due Diligence process.

Business readers will find the book so informative that it becomes their 'bible'. Companies are all different from one another. So, as exit time approaches, detailed individual counselling will be essential, especially from your accountants. This book is not intended to undermine their specific advice, but it is designed to highlight aspects needing pre-sale deliberation and maybe some reconstruction, as part of your customised exit strategy.

'Prepare To Sell Your Company' is addressed to entrepreneurs and owner managers of Small to Medium Enterprises (SMEs). Thus it is appropriate to 75% of UK businesses.

It is written in an easy read style for busy executives and contains some unusual information, possibly contentious, but certainly interesting, since it is written by one with practical experience of preparing then triumphantly selling companies.

For brevity throughout the following chapters you will find references to 'him', 'he' or 'business man' which should be taken to refer to both men and women. And the many references to 'owner manager' refer to the 'principal', that is the person with the majority shareholding, who drives the company forward. He is frequently the managing director or chairman in an SME company. He is probably *you*.

Preparation for exit can take from three to five years or even longer.
Accountants advise planning your exit right from the first day in business.
There is no time to lose.
You should start today.

CHAPTER ONE

Early Considerations

In this chapter:

- *Selling your company*
- *Why you should make plans for your exit*
- *Your exit plans should bring you these benefits*
- *The most influential factor, the P/E ratio, explained*
- *Buyers are either acquirers or investors*
- *Why should you sell your company?*
- *Traditional exit options explained*
- *Taking advice from professionals*
- *Who are these professional advisers?*
- *Selecting your corporate advisers*
- *The importance of secrecy*
- *The world of business hates uncertainty*

Selling your company

> Selling your company is a trying time, akin to selling your house. So much upset! For those unfamiliar with this process the challenging thoughts will be: 'How to go about it?' 'Who will help me?' 'How much to ask for the company?' 'Who will buy it?' 'When should I start?' 'How should I prepare?'

Relax

This book will answer your questions.

These pages will help you plan the most exciting period of your life.

Why you should make plans for your exit

Like all entrepreneurs, you will rightly feel proud of the business you have created. You probably believe that when the time comes to sell up or exit, your company will be attractive and strong enough to sell itself. You think that buyers will be falling over themselves to complete a purchase from you, at an outrageously high price.

No... This is rarely the case.

That is sad, because the proceeds from the sale of your company will often represent your pension, or capital to invest elsewhere.

Yet a programme to mould the business, to put into it all the factors and features that buyers and their financial supporters will look for, in addition to your turnover and profit, can produce an outstandingly attractive proposition.

> An exit strategy that grooms your business to show off its best features will handsomely reward you for the effort.

Your exit plans should bring you these benefits

◆ The highest possible sale price. This is achieved by grooming the company to become a desirable proposition.

◆ A company that will interest and be appealing to a very wide range of buyers, so the resultant auction mentality actually yields the maximum in sales proceeds.

◆ An exit timed to suit your own personal life plans.

- A **sale price** that is tax efficient, allowing you to legitimately retain more of the sale proceeds upon completion. In other words, pay as little tax as possible. This will only be achieved by forward planning.

- Obstacles that could impede a successful company sale have been removed.

- Time-wasting purchasers on 'spying trips' are discouraged. Genuine buyers only.

- Only buyers with sufficient financial resources to proceed to sale completion will be engaged in discussions.

- Refunds to buyers following the sale are mitigated, thus giving you peace of mind. Following the sale you can keep it all.

- Stress for you and your fellow shareholders is eliminated because the pathway to a sale is smoothed.

Take note
Exit preparations are complex, needing up to five years to develop.
Now is the time for you to *think big*. It is the ordinary person **who plans** who *will become a millionaire*.
So whatever stage your business is at today, you should set about preparing for exit **now**.

But first
For those of you new to selling businesses you must learn about the most influential factor in selling a company:
P/E ratio

The most influential factor, the P/E ratio, explained

> 'P/E ratio'...............'The multiple'..............'The multiplier'

P/E ratio, the multiple, or multiplier are terms used when calculating a company valuation. Whilst these accountancy terms have different meanings (see Glossary) they all arrive at the same **number,** and the same conclusion, which is a number that represents informed opinion of:

A company's risk factors, growth potential and industry sector comparisons.

This number is used to multiply your after tax profit figures to give a company valuation.

> **P/E ratio at work**
> Company annual profit (after tax)   × P/E ratio   = company valuation
> Say £500,000   × say 7   = £3,500,000

> Now you can see the influence of the P/E ratio.
> See how it boosts your company valuation.
> The P/E ratio is the single most significant factor in preparing a company for sale.
> You should aim for a high P/E ratio.

> There are various other ways to calculate company valuation.
> See Chapter 2, p53.
> But in the end the only true valuation is what a buyer will pay you.

Buyers are either acquirers or investors

Acquirers, **or purchasers**, are companies or individuals who buy a business in order to own it and run it themselves, often merging it with another company in their ownership. Their interest is focused on running and expanding the business, as well as making profit.

> Acquirers are frequently backed by financial investors. Your business will have to impress them as well as the acquiring company, or else the funds will not be forthcoming to buy your company.

Investors are investment companies or individuals who buy a business, but install someone to run it on their behalf. Generally, their interest is focused solely on gaining financial returns as both growth and profitability. After three, or five or even seven years they will generally sell your business to another investor, in order to crystallise the increased valuation and profit on their original investment in your 'old' company.

But first things first . . .

Why should your sell your company?

The answer to this question will help you choose the best exit route for *you*.

Reasons for you to sell your company

◆ The assets and value that have built up within your company will be released by a sale, producing wealth for you and fellow shareholders.

◆ A new opportunity/challenge has presented itself to you, even a new business interest perhaps? Selling the company will produce both capital to invest, and time to spend on the project.

- Sometimes your company's growth seems to require continuous financial support from you as the principal owner. You wish to bring this situation to an end.

- The fast rate of your company's expansion has outstripped your desire to stay in the business. Association with a larger company would be good for the business, and allow you to escape.

- Divorce/family breakdown has produced a need to access 'cash within' the business.

- Retirement beckons, or at least you need a reduction in your business commitments.

- For family companies, succession issues may be solved by a sale.

- If your health is poor you may be relieved of business stress.

- Any owner manager who feels out of his depth, bored or who has lost interest in the business he has created, can leave with honour.

- An ailing or declining business can sometimes be saved from bankruptcy or closure by a strategic company sale, whereas trading out of trouble seems impossible.

By understanding the benefits attached to each exit option it will be easier to decide on the most suitable exit for you.

Traditional exit options explained

Trade sale

This describes a circumstance where you and fellow shareholders sell the business to another company (often in a similar line of business), thereby relinquishing ownership. Payment of the negotiated sale price is made to you, sometimes all in cash, sometimes as a mixture of cash, plus shares in the acquiring company.

> It is a trade sale that is most likely to bring the greatest wealth to you and fellow shareholders. Trade buyers can afford to pay more. This is because they can cross fertilise with the other business(es) they own. This enables savings in running costs that feed down to increased profit, producing the funds to pay for the purchase of your company.

As a condition of sale, you may be asked to stay on in a consultancy role, to pass on company knowledge and 'know how', and introduce the new owners to the company's major customers. This role commands a fee for you because you are now acting as an employed consultant. However, if you have made yourself surplus to requirements by training an Executive Team to run the business without daily reference to you, then you could find that you are quickly allowed to leave.

See Chapter 5, page 91.

Sale to an investment company

A thriving business, with an abundance of future potential, a robust financial standing, plus a strong Executive Team will interest many investment companies. When an investment company buys a business it usually prefers to retain the incumbent management, to run the company on its behalf. It is possible that for a time you may be required to lead the company, just until their own senior executives settle in. But this time may be short if you have an Executive Team in place.

See 'Benefits of an Executive Team', page 93.

If you **do not have** an Executive Team of managers, then the investment company will want you to remain employed as an Executive Manager for an agreed period of time, following the sale.

Thus, you have sold your shareholding yet still have to attend work on a daily basis, receiving an additional negotiated reward (a salary package) for doing so. However, control and political direction of the company will remain with the investors (unless specific terms of engagement have been negotiated).

Earn outs, or contingent payouts

'Earn outs', 'contingent payouts' or 'contingency deals' are terms that describe your company being sold to purchasers who pay only **a part of the negotiated sale price** at completion. This arrangement is full of potential hiccups for you as owner manager.

- The outstanding part of the negotiated sale price is only paid to you and fellow shareholders if certain agreed targets are met.

- You, as owner manager, would usually remain in post to manage the company and steer it towards these targets.

Dangers that may lurk in earn outs/contingent payouts

- Firstly, only part of the sale price has been received by you.

- Secondly, you have not gained freedom from everyday work.

- Thirdly, you are unlikely to have control of the company, its strategy, politics or matters that could affect the successful attainment of those pre-set contingency targets. It is the new owners who will direct all strategies.

Earn outs
carry the danger that the contingency targets are never fully met, thus the remainder of the sale proceeds is never paid out to you.
This exit option is the least favourable, unless very strong terms can be negotiated, which do, in effect, allow the target to be attained by your hard work. It is very rare for new owners to grant you the strength of control that you will need.

Sale to a family member

This involves a family business, and sale of the shares of the controlling shareholder (presumably you, the owner manager) to **a member of the family**.

There are a number of issues surrounding 'sales to family'. In the first place, the family members, even with all of their resources combined, are unlikely to be able to raise sufficient capital to buy you out at **full market value** without obtaining external financial investor support. Since you, the principal, have been the driving force behind the company, these supporting investors would be nervous about your departure. This exit could be full of undesirable complications.

If you have been far sighted enough to train up someone, or an Executive Team, to take your place in running the company, this action will have inevitably revealed your hope to exit. Thereafter, family feuds over seniority, favouritism, disagreement with your policies or other family squabbles may colour matters so that the company does not achieve its full financial potential, and a reduced sale price ensues.

Often, a trade sale will achieve far better sales proceeds. But planning to exclude family members from your exit programme will require considerable courage, and to be effective it will need a strong and probably long exit strategy.

> To attain a successful outcome, all planning for your exit must be kept secret.

Management Buy Out (MBO)

Management buy out describes the circumstance whereby a team of executive managers already employed in your company offers to 'buy out' you and all other shareholders.

Two schools of thought exist on management buy outs (MBOs). Firstly, this could offer an opportunity for a very secret and quick sale, since external companies do not need to be approached to measure the market interest. Plus the sale could be speedier than the norm because the management team know what they are buying into. Providing they have raised sufficient financial support, an MBO could be advantageous, whereas a trade sale may seem difficult and prolonged. An MBO may be an opportune solution if a sale needs to be completed urgently.

The second school of thought is that an MBO may not deliver the full and true company value. This is because the MBO team will have already been employed within your business in influential and authoritative positions and so have realised that your intention is to sell up. Given adequate time and opportunity they could have mustered sufficient financial backing to make a bid.

> It is quite common for a period of company stagnation to occur prior to an MBO bid, as the management buy out team's attention is focused on attaining funds and preparing the bid, rather than creating increased company turnover, profit and value. This would adversely affect the sale price that you and fellow shareholders are offered.
>
> Indeed, the MBO team will probably come to realise that by increasing the company turnover and thereby the company valuation, a higher sale price will ensue (thus costing them more).

Following an MBO, you, as departing owner manager, will generally be completely free to leave the company. Your warranties and guarantees to the purchasers could be reduced since the MBO team know the company's weaknesses and strengths and will be aware of any pending adversity.

See 'Warranties and Guarantees' in Glossary.

Management buy in (MBI)

This bears remarkable similarity to an MBO except that all of the managers buying in are external parties.

Buy in management buy out (BIMBO)

Once again, this is similar to a management buy out, except that in this case an external company managing director may team up with some of your existing company staff, to buy the company between them.

In this case, you will be required to give normal warranties and guarantees as part of the Due Diligence procedure.

Cease to trade

This exit is not the most effective route to riches, since the only

See 'Intellectual property', Chapter 8.

wealth gained is found in the liquidation of the company's saleable assets; disposing of equipment and property whilst collecting in outstanding debts.

But even this exit option can be vastly improved by making use of the very best experts in stock valuation and intellectual property values. 'Ceasing to trade' could be a solution if there are urgent personal reasons for an owner manager to leave his business: poor health, for instance.

If the business is no longer a going concern, then much of the asset value may have already disappeared. This may bring about bankruptcy, voluntary liquidation, or even an application made by a third party to wind up the company's affairs.

Ceasing to trade is best avoided if at all possible.

Flotation or listing on the London Stock Exchanges or Alternative Investment Market (AIM)

Flotation

In simple terms, flotation describes a scheme whereby the private company shareholders sell a percentage of the company's shares to the public. Subsequently, the shares are traded at the Stock Exchange. This takes the company out of private and into public ownership.

There are several stock exchanges. All are tightly regulated bodies, where strict financial and legal compliance is essential. Member companies are required to report publicly, quarterly, on their performance (for good or ill).

- Gaining any stock exchange listing would be a long, costly and arduous exit route for you to take, but it should be balanced against the very considerable rewards that may be gained, providing that the company is suitable for a stock exchange listing.

- Stock exchange membership requires large profit generation to be considered for listing, plus obvious and considerable **future profit potential** from its member companies. For businesses that have grown fairly large in both turnover and profit this could be an attractive option.

- Because you, as owner manager, have company expertise and experience you would be required to stay on and run the company.

- You would also be expected to continue holding a fair proportion of your company's shares, which the market sees as its security against company failure.

- So for you, the actual exit from daily work is delayed until a company structure that is acceptable to the new, public shareholders is achieved.

> You should obtain expert financial and legal advice before entertaining this awesome complicated and long-winded exit.

Taking advice from professionals

Now that you have reviewed the exit options and decided on the most appropriate for you, you'll discover that you are going to need professional advisers. It is a wise owner manager who selects a team of corporate advisers from a very early stage of company development (soon after start up is not too soon). You should then make use of their wealth of experience during the growth stages of the business and thereafter on to company sale.

Who are these professional advisers?

They are auditing accountants, corporate lawyers, corporate finance specialists, and the commercial arm of your bank, known as corporate bankers. Their specialist functions are explained below.

Auditing accountants

You should select a medium- or larger-sized accountancy practice of some standing, with a good reputation and experience of preparing accounts ready for a company sale. You will need them to prepare and audit your annual accounts, in the years prior to sale. They will also advise on the appropriateness and timing of your exit strategies, being especially concerned with tax planning issues. They will discuss the presentation of your accounts, especially how items in the balance sheet and the profit and loss accounts are moved around to maximise the value of the company. All of this takes place in the years prior to sale.

> You should resist the temptation to select a 'small time' accountancy practice, or a friend's practice. Choosing accountants who have actual experience of bringing companies to sale is crucial to the success of your exit strategy.

Corporate lawyers

Company law, together with regulation and law on disposals, mergers and acquisition, is very precise, and generally beyond the experience of the average domestic solicitor who will not be familiar with its fine detail. Even the business jargon used in the application of company law has been known to faze the 'high street' solicitor, who is often more used to family matters. The expense will be worthwhile. **Don't be penny pinching on this matter, you will regret it.**

A good corporate lawyer, **experienced in many company sales, is a** *must.* Otherwise, you may be exposed to serious risk, either from the deal collapsing or from agreeing to something that you should not have. **It is essential to select a corporate solicitor with an excellent reputation in company disposals**, whose references you have checked.

Corporate lawyer specialisms
Pre-sale preparation:

◆ Guidance is vital on the set up of your company. You should consult your lawyers to find the most suitable company constitution for you, and then they will prepare all of the appropriate documentation.

◆ At times of company growth, and when substantial expansion capital is needed, your lawyers will advise you on the most appropriate schemes, constructing on your behalf all the paperwork involved.

◆ Your lawyers will spot and rectify any area of non compliance with company regulation and law.

◆ Should you decide to mount a 'shares buy back', prior to your company sale, support from your corporate lawyers will be essential.

See 'Shares buy back', Chapter 14.

At sale time:

◆ Your company lawyers work in tandem with your corporate finance specialists to create the best deal for your circumstances.

◆ As soon as an offer is made for the company, your lawyers take over, to shoulder the burden of all legal matters. This includes the Heads of Agreement, Due Diligence examination, disclosures, warranties, guarantees, indemnities and the preparation of the mountains of documentation in connection with the sale process.

◆ Your corporate lawyers have access to barristers for advice on points of law, should they feel that it is necessary.

> See 'Due Diligence', Chapter 16.

> Using corporate lawyers to conduct negotiations ensures you will be fully legally protected from after sale litigation. Meanwhile, you are free to participate in Due Diligence, whilst your Executive Team keep the company running to target.

Where can you find corporate lawyers?

Corporate lawyers are to be found via the Internet, *Yellow Pages*, trade organisations, CBI, Institute of Directors and the Federation of Small Businesses. Banks are often able to indicate the names of several companies but are unlikely to recommend to you any specific practices.

It is a good idea to use lawyers who come to you well recommended and these you will find through networking. The lawyers you select should be from a **specialist corporate department** of a large practice. Ask to see lists of deals they have concluded and take up references.

Corporate finance specialists

These are specialist accountancy practices (or divisions of large accountancy practices), solely concerned with conducting company disposals, mergers and acquisitions. So they have all the expertise that you are going to need. These knowledgeable professionals are exceptionally valuable to you **prior to sale** as well as during negotiations, as the following information demonstrates.

Your corporate financiers' pre-sale advice:
- Working in tandem with your auditing accountants they will help you with your essential pre-sale tax preparations, to include all aspects of personal and business tax planning.

- Prior to sale, they will offer you business expansion advice geared to the fact that you are hoping to sell the company.

- They can introduce you to private equity funds or other financial support wherever capital injection is advantageous to you.

- They are able to provide company valuation services, linked to your company sale.

- They can involve the Government Pension Regulator to examine your company pension scheme(s) with the object of issuing clearance on it. This absolves you from future troubles and is a crucial step in any sale. Your auditing accountants can also arrange this for you.

- In tandem with your auditing accountants they can offer pre-sale guidance on positioning your company's financial structure and statements to advantage.

At sale time:
- Corporate financiers will 'head up' the proceedings for you, leaving you free to keep the business running.

- They will prepare the Information Memorandum, an in-depth company prospectus that gives acquirers/investors the details and data they need to make a decision on whether or not to proceed to sale negotiations.

◆ However good you are at selling, you should leave the business of selling your company to your corporate finance specialists.

◆ They will negotiate with your acquirer/investor and will structure the deal type that gives you best advantage. Because they understand the nuances of deal structures, they will endeavour to protect you from all problems, whilst liaising with your corporate lawyers, financial backers and banks.

◆ Their neutrality means that no one's feelings will be hurt when the purchaser makes adverse comments about your company, which is all part of the process of the purchaser trying to reduce the deal price.

◆ They are skilled in seeking and anonymously finding acquirers or investors. This is accomplished in such a fashion that the search does not impact on the ongoing integrity of your business.

◆ They are able to anonymously establish a potential buyer's credit worthiness, discovering very early on whether he has the ability to raise sufficient funds to complete the sale, then politely eliminating unsuitable buyers.

◆ They are able to discover whether a potential acquirer has a genuine intention to buy or whether his approach is bluff intended to achieve a 'spying trip'. People who prove to be not genuine buyers will be excluded from the sale preliminaries at a very early stage, before any sensitive and confidential information and data are revealed.

◆ Corporate financiers have databases of clients who could be interested in your company. This may be useful if you have not yet found a buyer or the original purchaser drops out.

Where can you find corporate finance specialists?
Corporate finance specialists can be found from the same sources as corporate lawyers: *Yellow Pages*, trade organisations, the Internet, CBI, Institute of Directors, the Federation of Small Businesses and your bank's introduction. But, once again, networking and personal reference is the best source. Ask to see lists of clients they have advised throughout a company disposal, and take up references.

Should you use corporate finance specialists from the same firm as your auditing accountants?
◆ There may be some advantages in your doing so. Alternatively, you may feel it is better to use separate companies.

◆ You should make the decision on the experience of the corporate finance specialist company.

◆ They should have a successful track record in numerous deals of your size. Check out the questions to ask in 'Selecting your corporate advisers'.

Commercial division of your bank

When a company turnover has grown to a reasonable figure, banking should be embarked upon with the business division of your bank rather than via the high street bank manager. Further growth will take you to the commercial division. For everyday trading, deposits and withdrawals can still be transacted via the high street branch, but your commercial bank adviser can offer a much wider range of business support services than can be accessed via any high street bank manager. The guidelines are very approximate in this:

- start up to approximately £100,000 turnover – high street branch manager;

- £100,000 turnover (or lower but showing fast growth potential) – business manager;

- £1 million turnover upwards – commercial division.

You are looking for the division of the bank that deals with 'levered' or 'structured' transactions regularly.

The benefits of dealing with the commercial banking division
- Commercial bankers readily understand the world of business decisions, expansion opportunity and risk. They have the authority to grant you higher levels of borrowing than the high street branch manager.

- They understand about 'cash flow' lending, as well as security-focused lending.

- Business support facilities and schemes are available to you via your commercial banking division.

- If you need long- or short-term financial assistance for your business, this is readily understood and various schemes from the bank or elsewhere will be discussed with you.

- You may wish to use their invoice discounting/factoring services to assist in your company's cash collection.

- When planning your long-term strategies, access to information from the banks' economic forecasters is invaluable.

- Banks are usually brilliant at organising networking functions (breakfast meetings, conferences, etc). These provide you with excellent opportunities for business and personal development.

- Your commercial banking advisers are acquainted with most corporate lawyers and corporate finance specialists already. They are used to working with these professionals as part of the adviser team that a wise owner manager assembles around himself.

Dealing with your commercial bank

- You will be assigned your own account manager, who will grow to understand you and everything concerned with your business and your aspirations.

- Most commercial bank managers are target driven to retain business clients like you, and assist in your company growth.

- Your requests for financial assistance will be appraised as a component of the company's development strategy.

- Any risk factors in your business will be of prime consideration to the bank. It is your robust risk management policies that will impress your bank. They often adjust their charges and interest rates proportionate to perceived risks, where high risk equates to higher interest rates.

- Your commercial bank will be impressed by your careful and sensible money management, your credit control strategies, your detailed financial management account reporting and financial forecasting. This spells out your professionalism that will influence your banking terms.

- You should discuss bank charges with your bank every year, noting the criteria used to calculate these charges. It is a recommended practice to conduct a competitive tendering process every two or three years. Surprisingly, banks can 'adjust' their fees when faced with competition, reasoned argument and reduced risk policies. You will find everything is negotiable.

- Obtaining financial support by using your house and home as collateral is a dangerous practice. You should explore the many other options of obtaining security, refusing as far as possible to pledge your home. Frequently your account manager can assist you with this hurdle.

  > Pledging your house as security is a dangerous move. Frequently, other securities can be negotiated.

- You should check out your account manager. Building a rapport with him will be an important feature of a successful banking partnership. During preliminary discussions there are some factors worth asking him about that will assist in promoting a successful relationship. For instance: How many clients does he handle? Is he managing, or does he have any ties with any of your competitors?

- Evaluate his time pressures and his commitment to *you*, as his client.

- You should insist on meeting your account manager's boss, as part of effective networking. Should you ever find yourself happy with the bank, but uncomfortable with your account manager, insist upon another person within the bank to deal with your business affairs.

◆ Your bank, along with all of your professional contacts, will make judgements on your business acumen, which will be used in all aspects of your dealings with them.

> Do not be afraid of banks, even if you are borrowing from them. Without clients like you they would not be in business. They should become your friend, and part of your trusted advisory team.

Selecting your corporate advisers

Your choice of corporate advisers could be crucial to a good exit operation. Once again it is advised that the selection process should take place **a long time before you exit**. Building a team of advisers, all of whom understand one another and others' ways, is a vital ingredient rarely mentioned.

> An efficient team of professional advisers can enhance the outcome of sales negotiations.

Look out for friendliness, or conversely antagonism, towards one another. You would need to address this latter situation, well before exit.

The process of adviser selection will produce many questions that you should ask candidates, so it is best to hold a 'beauty parade', with the same queries being addressed to all contenders. Let each know that he has competitors, so that you can get sensibly priced quotations and terms.

Explain to each what you are trying to achieve. Let them review both an audited set and a management set of accounts. Tell them your preferred exit timescale if this been decided.

> Any company that will not take part in this competitive
> selection process should not be considered.

A few guide questions are listed here to help you

◆ How many company disposals have you done?
This is a 'must' question since you are buying their 'know how'
of having accomplished other company sales. Choose only
those with considerable practical experience of company
disposals.

◆ What can your company do for me?
Detailed verbal and written company profiles are essential.
Don't be put off with 'What would you like?' It is their job to
tell you what they can do for you.

◆ What are your charges, and the basis of calculation of those
charges?

◆ Do you undertake work where payment is contingent upon a
successful outcome?
In other words, no sale, no fee. Most large practices will
accept this basis. But others who will not undertake these
terms may be unfamiliar with sales processes (not your best
choice), or have assessed **you as a high risk client** who is
unlikely to easily conclude a sale. Find out which it is.

◆ During negotiation how do you support me?

◆ Can you find buyers for my business? How do you go about
doing so?

◆ Can you produce references from your past customers,
particularly those that you have advised on company exits?

You should follow up these references tactfully, since you do not want to broadcast too soon the fact that you are selling up.

> Although all advisers will tell you that they can deal with 'any size of transaction', in practice they do seem to have specialities. Press this point to see if they are more used to dealing with say £10 million, £50 million, £200 million deals. Select the one dealing in your category.

In making judgements you need these questions answered:

◆ How well did he do in 'selling' his company's services to me? Remember he will be 'selling' your company, for you.

◆ Will these advisers do all that I want them to do?

◆ Is their reputation good?

◆ Do I like the individual enough to work with him during a really stressful time?

◆ If you feel uncomfortable with an adviser, but like the company he represents, then be straightforward in requesting another person within the practice to advise you.

Fees

As well as your bank, both your corporate lawyers and your finance specialists are amenable to adjusting their fees – in other words, tendering. These professional costs will accrue dependent on the size, the valuation and possibly the complexity of the deal involved in your sale.

But, if your company is adequately groomed for sale, then competent advisers will gain the best market price. In other words, **their fees will be worthwhile**. Good references from their clients are a guideline that should be balanced against fees.

The importance of secrecy

Exit preparations take a very long time. During this prolonged period, 'open discussion' with people within your company on the subject of your exit, or 'a company sale', must be avoided at all costs, since a climate of uncertainty will otherwise have been introduced.

To those who are not used to the business world it seems strange that your exit plans need to be shrouded in secrecy. But they must. Why is this so? The answer follows.

The world of business hates uncertainty

- During times of uncertainty, or rumour, **company shareholders** become nervous about the safety of their investment. This lack of confidence could lead them to try to sell their shares, or to reduce their investment in your company, thus causing a crisis of funding.

- Whenever a business is rumoured to be for sale, **the company's customers** become worried that their continuity of supply will fail, or that the standards of product or service they are receiving will be adversely affected. This worry may cause them to cancel their orders and contracts (or fail to renew contracts), thereby reducing your company's sales turnover and future order book.

- Speculation of takeover may affect **suppliers** who become concerned that the new owners will fail to pay outstanding invoices, or will discontinue trading operations. In their efforts to discover whether there is cause for concern, they gossip randomly thus perpetuating a problem.

◆ Whispers of possible new ownership can affect **employees** who become frightened about continuity of employment, changes in workplace practice, or financial reward. This may lead them to seek employment elsewhere, thus leaving the company shorthanded at a time when a stable workforce is vital. Losing key members of staff can be damaging because they are bound to take sensitive company information with them, to their new employers.

> **Gossip**
> about your company sale can damage your company
> and damage your plans.

◆ Worse still, if **competitors** get to hear of a takeover in the pipeline, they could contact your existing customers, creating chaos and crises of confidence, probably leading to a downturn in trade.

◆ Loss of business, and loss of confidence in the company's future performance, means that it will be seen as a dubious acquisition. All of this suspicion could destroy a deal. In the worst case scenario, the company could actually fold, because so much mischief has been done.

◆ Last, but not least, courtesy must be given to acquirers/ investors, who for perfectly good commercial reasons may not wish to broadcast their interest in your company.

> So whilst you are preparing the company for a sale it is important to maintain silence on the subject, keeping all plans a secret to yourself.

Next steps

You have taken a preliminary look at the matter of selling your company. Now is the time to become aware of some of the other important influencing factors around a sale, in particular your own ambitions and aspirations for your future.

CHAPTER TWO

Major Factors that Influence Exit

In this chapter:

- *Influencing factors that you should know about*
- *What acquirers/investors look for*
- *Getting the best sales proceeds*
- *Identifying potential acquirers/investors*
- *Your personal aspirations*
- *What to look for when selling the company*
- *Setting your exit package*
- *Tip on tax*
- *Company valuation using the P/E ratio/multiplier method*
- *Increasing your company valuation*
- *Deductions from the sales proceeds*
- *Distribution of sale proceeds amongst shareholders*
- *Is this enough for your exit package?*
- *Further company valuation methods*

Influencing factors that you should know about

Knowing what purchasers look for will help you to mould your company, so that it is attractive to a wide range of potential buyers, thus increasing the likelihood of sale completion at a good price.

So what attracts them? What puts them off? What makes them pay high prices? What gives grounds for low prices?

The answers to these questions give you the opportunity to introduce attractive features and eliminate any unsatisfactory elements within your business.

What acquirers/investors look for

Genuine acquirers/investors will probably already have done some preliminary checking you out, prior to any discussion.

Your personal reputation interlinked with the company's activities will have been scrutinised via trade associations, gossip, banks, accountants and the like. Companies House will have been approached for your last three years' accounts.

> Each acquirer/investor will seek something different from the purchase of your company.

Risk-free acquisition

Every purchase carries some degree of risk, but acquirers/investors will want to know that the risk factors involved in buying/investing in your company are minimal. Buyers will be frightened off by any threats to the future stability of the company.

Read about 'Due Diligence', Chapter 16.

Buying a company, with all of the associated costs, requires some 'pay back', or 'return on investment' (ROI) for the acquirer/investor. Therefore, buyers look for companies with a stable and secure future, together with the opportunity to increase both the turnover and the profit of the business, with as little risk as possible.

Low risk, high growth potential deserves high P/E ratio.

Investment opportunity

An investment buyer will appoint managers to run the company on their behalf following the company sale. So, they are looking for a sound business, with plenty of growth potential, and good profit figures. Having completed the purchase from you and your fellow shareholders, they will usually own the company for the next three to seven years, building its size and profitability. Then, by selling it, they will capitalise on its increased size, value and profit. This capital gain will then fund re-investment elsewhere. During this time they will have introduced and trained up their own executives to run the company. Initially, you may be asked to assist in this aspect.

If your business has high growth potential and good profitability it could command a high P/E ratio from investment companies.

Growth, procured by acquisition

An acquirer can increase his own existing business turnover at a stroke, when buying a competing company. In purchasing your business he is eliminating a competitor from the field at the same time as increasing his growth. So, for him, an acquisition is a worthwhile investment, provided there are no objections from the Competition Commission and any risk factors are low.

Generally, such a trade buyer would be prepared to pay a higher price for your business than a financial investor. This is because cost savings can be made in the merger by stripping out superfluous overheads, and by bulk buying supplies.

Selling to a competitor should produce a high P/E ratio.

> A trade sale to a competitor will probably bring the highest sale price.

Acquisition of a sought after, popular brand named product(s)

This could refer to a range of products or services known by its brand name, owned by your company and having full intellectual property protection. If acquisition of your branded product can only be accomplished by purchase of your entire company, then a company sale is likely to ensue.

See 'Second tier sale' in Glossary.

Or maybe you would consider selling the brand itself in a 'second tier sale'?

See 'Intellectual assets', Chapter 8.

Developing a brand and successfully marketing to a wide range of clientele is a time-consuming and expensive exercise, calling for 'hands-on' marketers. Acquisition eliminates all of the time and cost involved. Acquisition of a popular brand can bring kudos plus speedy financial returns.

This gives grounds for a high P/E ratio.

Acquisition of intellectual property (intellectual assets)

Many companies are acquired for their ownership of particularly desirable items of intellectual property (IP). This is different from a brand name (although brand names are intellectual property) in that copyright, design rights, trade marks, patents, licences, etc, even 'rights to produce', may be involved. Occasionally, the IP concerned is in cold storage, not yet having been marketed by its owners, for all manner of reasons, usually financial. But an acquisitive company may covet the potential returns that the ownership of these IP rights could bring, and so wish to own them for itself.

Sometimes, an acquirer wishes to own the items of IP to keep them secret, and simply prevent them ever reaching the public domain, thus to stop them competing with his own product.

See 'Intellectual property and assets', Chapter 8.

If your company owns special designs, patented products, or even just the patents themselves, plus any other intellectual asset, this can be a very valuable acquisition.

High P/E ratios should transpire.

Acquisition of the company's name

When the name of the company is well known, with an enviable reputation (perhaps acting as a brand), an acquirer may wish to buy just the company name on its own, as a separate entity, without buying the actual trading company itself. This is a very strong sale, which accountants describe for obvious reasons as 'second tier sale', producing generous additional revenue.

In this circumstance, you are probably making two sales to two separate buyers:

1. selling the company name with its associated reputation;

2. selling the business entity itself.

So, developing a company's name and its good reputation should prove a major feature in your exit strategy.

This can command a good P/E ratio.

> See Chapter 8
> Intellectual assets and how to develop, protect and promote them
> prior to sale thereby increasing the P/E ratio.

Acquisition of a young 'up-to-the-minute' trendsetting product range

Any new, eye-catching trendsetting product(s) with potential for vast market penetration will be coveted by acquisitive company bosses. If obtaining the product(s) is only achieved by buying your company you are in a strong position. Once again, pay attention to any IP protection issues. Ensure also that the product has not reached market saturation and is still in a growth phase.

> Ensure that the product range still has a lot of potential for growth.

For this a high P/E ratio can be anticipated.

Acquisition of marketplace control

A company supplying unique containers, dispensers, equipment or machinery, matched with sustained repeat order consumables to be used with your equipment, and available **only** from your company, is a valuable acquisition.

Marketplace control should bring you high P/E ratio.

Acquirers/investors dislike fickle/late payers

Avoid building your company clientele amongst the market segments that are fickle payers. Buyers are not keen on credit risk problems, and probably will walk away from the deal if there are such difficulties.

Check out credit ratings. Minimise credit risk. Don't take chances.

Acquirers/investors like a lot of customers who order regularly

In most companies the 80/20 (Pareto's) rule will be in play. That is: 20% of your customers produce 80% of company income.

Build a large customer base.

Increase the number of your clients to reduce the dangers related to heavy reliance on any particular customer, and to increase the number of clientele in your 20% Pareto band.

> There is very considerable risk in trading with too few clients.
> Suppose you lose some of them?
> As a general rule, no single client should bring in more than 20% of the company income.

Ensure that your clients place orders regularly with you, rather than your competitors. This boosts your turnover, and gives you opportunities to introduce additional products to them, which bolsters client loyalty.

Widespread market coverage, via lots of loyal clients, increases your turnover and is strongly appealing to buyers.

This should have positive influence on the P/E ratio.

Acquisition to gain entry to special markets

Gaining approved supplier status to some marketplaces can be difficult to achieve. Tricky entrance procedures, protracted tender applications, special IT software changes, exclusive product/service arrangements and client specific delivery terms or arrangements, may be involved. Examples of such clients requiring special arrangements are the NHS, armed forces, royal palaces and groups of especially large industrial companies.

For some companies the quick route to gaining such clientele may be via acquisition of those suppliers already holding current mandate or contract to supply products/services.

> These types of clientele are generally difficult to break into. But having awarded long supply contracts, they are difficult to 'lose'. However, ensure you are not too dependent upon too few of these clients. Having too few clients of any sort will always impact negatively on the P/E ratio.

**High P/E ratio is found in having many such contracts
with lots of time still to run.**

Acquisition of a significant property portfolio

If your company owns property located in geographical areas of special significance, this can increase your company valuation. It is sometimes possible to sell the property as a separate deal. Of course this may mean relocation.

You should take informed advice as to which is your best course of action. Significant 'second tier' business may result.

High P/E ratio here.

Acquisition of your sales methods and sales staff

Strong and effective sales teams and sales methods are valuable in their own right. Building a successful sales organisation, whether it is field sales, telesales, mail order (with catalogues), an online set up that works efficiently, or some other means of creating sales, will take time and is fraught with expense and problems. It involves constant training, and recruitment of both sales staff and managers, until success is finally achieved. There will be buyers who could think it worthwhile to acquire your company to circumvent the process of building their own sales organisation.

High P/E ratio could be charged for a ready-made successful sales operation.

Acquisition of your company 'know-how'

Technical companies operating in unique or particular fields will have specialised knowledge which may be difficult or nearly impossible to attain through 'normal' channels. Such instances are scientific companies, technical subjects or companies with newly developed specialised software.

High P/E ratios are a must for this type of company.

Acquisition of accreditations (internationally recognised)

Arguably this could be considered part of your intellectual property. As trade requires more and more regulation, it may be crucial to have particular accreditations, enabling trading with particular market segments. However, the gaining of such accreditations requires whole company 'special disciplines' and regular inspections by accreditation panels. Rarely is initial accreditation attainment an easy or quick matter, and there are companies whose methods of working would mean that they would never gain compliance with the accreditation standards. Purchase of ready made accreditations is usually impossible. But to buy a company operating in the approved fashion, with accreditations already in place, will be very attractive. Many accreditations are recognised internationally these days.

Holding such accreditations can contribute to a high P/E ratio.

Acquisition of speciality

This covers a multitude of possibilities. It could be a particularly cost effective supply chain management system, logistics operation, impressive cash generation method, desirable contracts, international trade, specialist knowledge, and so on. Anything which a buyer would have to spend time and money on developing to your standard could well be of interest.

This can command a high P/E ratio.

> Acquirers/investors look for low risk investment with potential for growth.

What about profit? Isn't that interesting to acquirers/ investors?

Yes, indeed it is. Some acquirers will view it as of prime importance. But each buyer will have his own reasons for looking at your company, and each will have a different view on profit according to his business.

> All buyers will be interested in profit figures that are steadily climbing year on year. This indicates good potential, forming an attractive proposition.

There are several other aspects of profit that will be closely interrogated.

Gross profit margins
These are of very special interest if yours are noticeably higher than the norm in your industry sector. Buyers would want to know how this is achieved and if it can be improved by their acquisition of the business.

High net profit returns could attract high P/E ratio

> Future profit enhancement opportunities, following acquisition, could lead to high P/E ratio. These may be attained by merger of your operations with the acquirer's current business. Or by property divestment, elimination of some director remuneration, reduction of staff, bulk buying of supplies, and so on.
> All of this leads to boosted profit that attracts buyers and influences the P/E ratio.

Using the projected profit figures in your company Information Memorandum, an acquirer/investor will calculate how many years it will take to recover the outlay involved in the purchase. Good profit generation, plus the opportunity to enhance the said profit after takeover, is a key factor in their decision to purchase.

> High P/E ratios should ensue for high profit potential.

Some other reasons for acquisition of a company
◆ The opportunity for a foreign investor to gain a foothold in the UK.

◆ Opportunity for an acquirer to diversify into new business activity.

> An acquirer will analyse the synergies between his existing business and the company that is for sale. He will examine any advantage he may gain, by asking the question 'What's in it for me?' So your company is worth more to some buyers than it is to others.

Getting the best sales proceeds

> To gain maximum sale value you should make your company 'well rounded' and desirable for as many reasons as possible. In doing so it becomes attractive to a broad band of acquirers/investors, allowing you an opportunity to seek out the highest bidder.

Sell the company before it has reached its peak
Every company, every product, every brand has a peak of perfection. It is best to sell your company before these peaks are achieved, so that a prospective purchaser can see there is a lot of potential business left to gain. Contracts should have plenty of time to run before they come up for renewal.

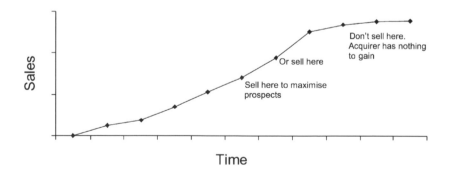

Figure 1. Sell before the company reaches its peak.

Identifying potential acquirers/investors

As you read through the reasons why acquirers/investors may buy a company, you will find that some potential bidders come readily to mind. But the wider your net is cast, the better your chances of a successful sale. Look at the possibilities.

- Competitors and companies already in your type of business.

- Companies, from a wide range of other industries, seeking to diversify.

- Suppliers seeking to reach your marketplace, **directly,** rather than through other companies like your own. Your business offers a ready-made vehicle for that aim.

- Overseas companies seeking a foothold in the UK.

- Financial institutions seeking an investment opportunity.

- Members of your staff who band together to form a management team in order to buy you out (an MBO).

- Other strong management teams from external sources who could effect a 'buy in management buy out' (BIMBO).

- Individuals that you have met during networking opportunities. These may come from a wide variety of backgrounds.

Pass all of the listed names to your corporate finance specialist.

> You have looked at acquirers/investors to see who they are and what they want. You have looked at the exit options.
> So the next step is to look at *you*.

Your personal aspirations

> Owner managers are usually an energetic breed, ambitious and often impatient. So pause for thought, at this stage, to consider your future aspirations. Some personal analysis is needed, together with some questions asked regarding your motives, before proceeding to make any plans. A time for reflection, you could say.

What do you want to do after the sale?

◆ Start up a completely new business venture?

◆ Purchase a new home, holiday or other property, boat, etc?

◆ Live abroad, or travel widely?

◆ Make substantial gifts to family or others?

◆ Donate generously to charitable causes?

◆ Make investments?

◆ Follow an expensive and perhaps time-consuming hobby?

◆ Retire and live off company sales proceeds?

◆ Obtain wealth, yet still remain working in either a full-time or part-time capacity?

◆ Other ideas, schemes.

> Decisions made now regarding your future lifestyle will enable a suitable sales deal to be completed at a time of your choosing.

What to look for when selling the company

It will seem obvious to you that selling your principal asset should be aimed at bringing substantial reward. So having worked and negotiated that 'dream deal' it is important to **keep** as much of it as possible. And the deal should not impinge on your future plans. So consider:

- **Your sales proceeds must be tax efficient.** Taxation is a major constituent of any sale and could involve huge sums of money. Tax efficiency can be affected by your age, the timing of the sale, the type of sale finally settled upon, plus a host of other personal factors. So your deal should have elements of tax efficiency built in.

   Input from tax advisers is essential a long time before exit.

- **Your sales proceeds must provide sufficient capital for your future needs.** Analysis of your ambitions for the future will tell you how much money you need to take away from your exit. So you should conduct an in-depth look at your personal wish list, setting down a realistic sum to cover all your plans (your exit package).

- **All your pension fund arrangements must be safeguarded.** The state of company pension funds will form a major feature of a buyer's decision as to whether to go ahead with this acquisition/investment or not.

Buyers will look for 'under funding', especially if the pension is a final salary scheme. The pension fund is also important to you since it will play an important part in your future 'incomings' at some time in your life.

   Pension experts are a *must* well before exit.

◆ **The sale should take place at a time of your choosing.** Having a sale forced upon you before you are ready could remove tax benefits, other financial benefit and possibly even social advantage. Conversely, a delayed sale risks coming to market when the company is past its peak.

Ensure that you build and maintain a strong financial status.

> **However,** the best time for **you** to exit may not always be the ideal time for the company to be sold. So give great consideration to which is the more important: your personal preferred exit time, or the best time as far as the market is concerned?
> **Consider why this is so before making a decision.**
> In an ideal world, your preferred time and the best time for the market place should be one and the same.

How much will it cost to fulfil your post-sale dreams?

If the sale of your company is to finance the next stage of your life you need to know fairly precisely the sum involved in the next stage of your life.

Put down on paper, in a cold calculated fashion, how much cash is required. Use fairly accurate figures, or at least generous over-estimates. Be realistic, since this is the amount that you will wish to take from the sale (the sale proceeds). Remember to add on at least 30%–40% to this figure to allow for contingencies.

> **Let's call this your exit package.**
> Think positively, it is absolutely possible to achieve your exit package with targeted preparation. You can drive through any deal if you have ruthlessly prepared the ground.

Setting your exit package

£££ personal expenditure to fulfil your dreams
plus
£££ personal debts and taxes to be (re)paid
plus
30%–40% contingency = exit package

Example calculation of desired exit package

Holiday home purchase	£300,000
Gifts to family	£100,000
Pay off mortgage, cards and debts	£500,000
Investments to produce future income	£1,000,000
Total exit package needed	**£1,900,000**
Add on contingency figure 40%	£760,000
Total exit package needed	**£2,660,000 net of tax**

Note: This exit package example does not contain provision for any **tax charges**. With accountants' advice you will need to add in an amount to cover all taxes due to HMRC as a result of the company sale.

Remember your exit package is the figure that you want to receive in sales proceeds.

Tip on tax

The tax rules are constantly changing, and each person's circumstance is uniquely affected, so it is best to take up-to-date personal advice from your tax adviser. Consult on all the aspects of your current and proposed financial affairs, with special regard to income tax liabilities, allowances, pensions and capital gains tax that are likely to be in effect at the time you hope to be selling. For some people, especially family companies, inheritance tax will assume particular importance. All of this will impact on the sum you will be required to pay to HM Revenue & Customs. Equally, the tax rules may well determine the most or least favourable time for your exit via sale. Be warned, taxation is of huge importance in the sale of a company, and may govern negotiations. Consultations with accountants should forewarn you of any post-sale obligations.

So what is the next step?

Calculate the value of your company as it stands today. What is it worth? Will it bring me in sufficient to produce my exit package if I sold up today?

Company valuation using the P/E ratio/ multiplier method

For this exercise we will look at the most commonly used method, the P/E ratio/multiples method that accountants use, called formula for the 'earnings valuation' of a business. This method seems a good rule of thumb, so to speak. **It is to be used only as a rough guide.**

You will need some idea about the P/E ratios that your industry sector has been producing in recent company disposals. What have recent companies sold for? This information is available via networking, accountants, business and trade organisations.

Formula for the earnings valuation of a business
Important information

The following demonstration formula uses for its example a post tax P/E ratio of multiple 7.

Your business may attain a higher or lower figure, but we will use 7 (an 'average' figure) in our demonstration.

Corporation tax used in this demonstration is an estimated figure (30%). This is subject to governmental change, so needs validation. In this example no allowance is made for other tax.

Core debt as used in this demonstration refers to the core, long-term borrowings, such as mortgage, borrowings from venture capitalists, business angels, permanent overdraft or discounting facilities that are never repaid. Trade creditors are not considered 'core debt'. Your core debts will be depicted in your balance sheet. The 'formula' below will produce only an approximate valuation, a rule of thumb.

Cash at bank is savings on deposit or invested. It does not refer to cash used as working capital.

Remember, any company's true valuation is the figure that someone will pay for it.

That is to say, in this demonstration, the company is worth **£3,480,000 to all** of the ordinary shareholders, although the profit is only **£490,000** after tax. In a sale situation the sale proceeds of

---

Formula for the earnings valuation of a business

Example

Net operating profit after interest and tax – say	£700,000
Deduct corporation tax – say 30%	£210,000
This gives 'notional profit after tax' (NPAT)	£490,000

Now apply P/E ratio (the multiplier) example, say 7

NPAT multiplied by P/E ratio = £490,000 × 7   **£3,430,000**

So your company valuation is £3,430,000

This demonstrates the tremendous effect of the P/E ratio, which has multiplied the company value from £490,000 to become £3,430,000.

Now:

Deduct core debt, say £400,000	£3,030,000
Add back cash at bank (savings not working capital) £450,000	£3,480,000
Deduct loan stock (preference shares) if any	NIL
Company valuation	**£3,480,000**

The total value of the company on a cash and debt free basis in this demonstration is £3,480,000

£3,480,000 will be divided amongst the shareholders, proportionally, by percentage shareholding entitlement and in accordance with the articles of association.

Increasing your company valuation

Imagine using the same NPAT figure £490,000 with a P/E ratio of, say, 9	
This would give £490,000 NPAT × P/E ratio 9	£4,410,000
Deduct core debt, say £400,000	£4,010,000
Add back cash at bank, say £450,000	£4,460,000
Deduct loan stock (preference shares)	NIL
Value of company on cash and debt free basis (nil loan stock) £4,460,000	

Just imagine...
Nearly £1,000,000 (£1 million) increase in company valuation just by applying a higher P/E ratio multiplier.

It is the abundance of desirable features that will improve your P/E ratio multiple.

> So aim for a high P/E ratio to increase your company valuation.

Further increased value can be obtained if you can make your profit figure higher **before you start your calculations**.
For instance, using the example on p48, if you currently take a salary of £200,000 p.a. and you know that you will not be needed by the new owners, then you can **add back** this amount into profit so that the £700,000 profit becomes £900,000 profit. Then continue with your equation, multiplying £900,000 (less corporation tax) × P/E ratio 7 and so on.

There may be some other **add backs**: some salaries; director costs; family salaries; bonuses; car or other assets costs in HP; interest charges; depreciation; and other non business costs currently paid for by your company.

The final outcome of your jottings will produce an 'on paper' exit package. This will trigger some ideas about the company's financial direction. For example, decisions about the sum of retained 'cash at bank' to improve company valuation, and whether or not you need to buy back your shares from financial backers to increase your profitability and shareholding, and hence your % of the sales proceeds. By what figure and in what timescale can you reduce or repay core debt? Consider also by how much, by what other means, and in what timescale, you can further improve profit.

Before setting about translating these paper figures into a reality you should play about with them until you can see what is possible and sensible. You should take into consideration deductions from the sales proceeds, and understand the procedure of distribution of the sales proceeds amongst fellow shareholders.

Deductions from the sales proceeds

In Chapter 1, you were strongly advised to make use of corporate advisers. These people will take you to success, but they need to be paid.

Commonly, they are content to await their payment until the deal has completed. Then, following completion, your lawyers will present you with a bill showing the combined amounts due to both lawyers and corporate financiers.

This sum will be deducted from your share of the total sale proceeds before distribution of the remaining proceeds to you and other shareholders. Your lawyers will reimburse your corporate financiers and other advisers accordingly.

Distribution of sale proceeds amongst shareholders

> Do you know your percentage shareholding and that of the other shareholders? This is strictly laid down by the number of shares held by each, and to some extent by their type. The facts ruling distributions are to be found in your articles and memorandum of association, especially if you have investors as shareholders.

Calculation of your percentage shareholding (assuming you have 'ordinary shares')

Example

The audited accounts show the allocation and entitlement of each shareholder. Percentage allocation is calculated thus:

Total company share capital, say £80,000

Perhaps you hold shares of, say £48,000

Thus your shareholding % $\dfrac{£48,000}{£80,000} \times 100 = 60\%$ shareholding

In plain English, if you hold £48,000 shares of total company shareholding of £80,000 **you have 60% shareholding.**

Distribution of sales proceeds explained

Assuming that your shares are ordinary shares, and you have 60% shareholding, then you are entitled to 60% of the total sale proceeds.

Example

Suppose total sale proceeds	**£6,000,000**
You are entitled to 60% of £6,000,000	**£3,600,000**

You will, however, **incur 60% of total professional fees**, which will be deducted from your sales receipts of £3,600,000 in the above example.

Sole shareholder
If you are a sole shareholder (there are no others), then you are entitled to the whole (100%) of the sale proceeds, after deduction of fees. You would incur 100% of the professional fees.

Preference shareholders
If your company has some preference shareholders (probably private equity or angels), they are usually entitled to their distribution of sales proceeds ahead of the ordinary shareholders. Once again your articles of association will reveal their entitlement.

Is this enough for your exit package?

Will the net sales proceeds from the company sale equate to the **exit package** that you are aiming for? Is it sufficient to cover all your plans and pipe dreams post sale? If not, then you must restructure the calculations until you gain the valuation that will bring your desired **exit package.** What profit figure should you aim for? What P/E ratio is needed?

> The most influential factor is the P/E ratio multiplier. If you make the company well rounded and extremely desirable your P/E ratio will increase. This in turn will multiply your profit to dramatically increase your sales proceeds.

Following this hypothetical calculation you must work to turn it all into reality.

Further company valuation methods

You should know that there are many methods of company valuation, especially if a company is loss making, close to 'break even in trading', or possesses a lot of assets. In paying out for an acquisition, the buyer looks at synergies and the specific value that he would gain from the purchase.

As we have already seen, some businesses are more valuable to particular buyers than others. All prospective purchasers are searching out the future potential of your business, and 'what's in it for him'.

> However, if you are looking for a precise and accurate company valuation, approach your corporate finance specialist, who can produce a more customised valuation, geared to your particular circumstance in the economic climate of the day.

Further valuation methods

Accountancy practices have many methods of measuring 'the worth' of a business. And each of them will be viewed from a different standpoint.

As the principal in your business you should keep an eye on your company valuation during growth. It is this figure that your bank and any agency will measure if you have to approach them for financial support. It would represent their security against a loan.

Help in valuing your business can be found via some software packages on the market that make claims to calculate these valuations.

Additionally, you may find the following methods are helpful. But remember that a company is only as valuable as the figure that someone will pay you for it. It is also worth noting that a buyer will value a company differently from a seller. This is where the negotiations begin.

Multiples method (earnings valuation of a business)
Earlier on in this chapter this method was viewed in depth. It is the most common method of evaluating a business, because it is the easiest to calculate and produces a broad brush valuation that is usable in exit planning.

Asset valuation method (book value)
◆ Your audited accounts will reveal the value of all of your company assets. By subtracting all of the company's liabilities, a figure emerges that is a very broad brush asset valuation.

◆ It would be difficult for you to use asset valuation in building an exit strategy since it takes no account of prospective future trade and profit.

◆ This method of valuation is not a true valuation, because there is no thought given to potential.

◆ Asset valuation literally measures tangible assets, only.

◆ Many companies' 'worth' is measured by their 'know-how', or expertise, in delivering their goods or services to their clients (not just their tangible assets). Asset valuation makes no provision for this.

For example: a publishing house has a few computers and office furniture as tangible assets. But its true value lies in its contracts with its authors, plus its skill in identifying potential 'blockbusters' and manuscripts that when published become bestselling books.

Discounted cash flow method (DCF)

This method of valuation could be hard to use when constructing an exit plan. It is based on the projected profit of the company, taken forward over a number of years into the future (usually the payback period that any buyer would expect). This sum is then discounted. That is, adjusted downwards to take account of the cost of inflation in future years, and the 'cost of money' in those future years, thereby arriving at a 'present value'.

Trade sale buyers will usually begin their valuation of your company with the discounted cash flow method, because they are aware of the synergies with companies they already own, and can foresee cost savings that could be made by combined buying power, combined trading costs and staff reductions, etc.

When planning your exit strategy discounted cash flow is *not* the best method to use, since there are too many unknown factors. It is usually considered a paper exercise; the P/E ratio valuation is more widely used in practice.

Break-up value

This is fairly obviously a method to avoid when planning your exit, since it is generally used if a company closes down. Whilst your accountants will have evaluated all your assets in your accounts, this can really bear no relation to actuality, where things will be sold at a knock down price.

Other valuation methods

Companies with unusual features may feel that special valuation methods should be used to establish a realistic view of their worth. Your auditing accountant can assist in this advice. He is certain to have a view on what factors will be influential in your company valuation.

Now you should go on to consider your exit strategy, which makes reality of your hypothetical figures and increases your P/E ratio.

CHAPTER THREE

Construct an Exit Strategy

In this chapter:

- *So you have made the decision to exit*
- *Factors that will help you decide your time plan*
- *Constructing your exit timetable*
- *Reviewing the facts before constructing your exit strategy*
- *Identifying your SWOTs*
- *Preparing your itemised exit strategy*
- *Taking your time*

So you have made the decision to exit

Having read the first two chapters of this book and decided that exit by company sale is what you want to do, you will need to begin your plan. That is, 'To build your customised strategy for exit'.

But first of all you must be aware of what you are letting yourself in for. It is a very lonely road you are about to travel. You can't reveal your hopes and plans to anyone, even your family. To everyone about you, you seem ruthless and manipulative. You'll have to take that on the chin.

It is hard work, with lots of 'out of hours' effort, maybe working away from the office. But it can be both exciting and rewarding to see the results of your ideas and the 'on paper project' becoming a reality. But to achieve your goal it is vital that you stay absolutely focused, and single minded in your efforts.

Factors that will help you decide your time plan

The actual timing of the sale is the single feature that can make the most difference to your sales receipts.

◆ You should review the general marketplace economics, and perhaps the country's political status. All of these can affect buyers' readiness to purchase, which reflects on P/E ratios. Bank economic forecasters are useful in preparation of long-term plans.

◆ In recessionary or depressed trading times, this is seen as a period of slow growth when plans for expansion are scaled back. Buyers find it more difficult to obtain funds to complete a purchase.

◆ Because taxation issues are of such significance it should figure amongst your first investigations. All aspects of company taxation plus all personal tax facets to include inheritance tax and capital gains tax will have impact on the most suitable exit date. Your accountants' advice is crucial in covering these aspects.

◆ Your personal circumstance will also have bearing on and may dictate the timing of the sale; for instance health, family commitment, etc.

◆ You may need time to regulate the company pension scheme.

- You should consider the length of time needed to introduce both a Corporate Constitution and a management structure.

- Bringing to perfection your product/service range may take some time.

- How long will it take you to develop an Executive Team (to replace yourself)?

- Consider the length of time needed to bring your company to its preferred financial status.

- Work out the 'pay back time' on core debt (loans from financial backers).

- How long do you need to develop, publicise and stabilise brands?

- How long will it take you to develop franchise operation to advantage?

- It is worth you taking a hard look at the state of your industry sector, noticing P/E ratios being achieved within the industry.

- Your own preferred exit date will probably influence your decision on your methods of achieving company growth and profitability. Quick routes are via acquisition, slower routes are organic growth.

Constructing your exit timetable

See Figure 2 'Exit time plan' on page 60.

- This diagram shows how to plan the basics. You will need to enter the factors connected with your own lifestyle that you consider relevant.

Date (end of financial year)	Owner manager's age and spouse's age	Project company turnover (t/o)	Projected net profit before tax plus % of t/o	Cash at bank	Remaining long-term debt
March 2009	OM's age 50 years Spouse's age 52 years	£1.9m	£175k 9.2% of t/o this year	£45k	£478k
March 2010	OM's age 60 years Spouse's age 53 years	£2.1m which is 10.5% increase on last year	£210k 10% of t/o this year	£79k	£400k
March 2011	?	?	?	?	?
March 2012	?	?	?	?	?

Figure 2. Exit time plan.

◆ Once you have developed your exit timetable it should form the basis of your exit strategy. Working out this complicated jigsaw will take you many attempts before a blueprint can be developed.

Reviewing the facts before constructing your exit strategy

Your exit strategy is another name given to the plans or 'to do' list you construct to bring the business into a state of readiness for sale.

> The exit strategy that you finally develop should be prepared by you alone, keeping its existence secret and confidential. Proposals, ideas and strategies within the programme could easily be misinterpreted and misunderstood, creating alarm within the workforce, if publicised.

Reading this book you will become aware that there are a great many features in your company that are so appealing that they have a really positive impact on the P/E ratio. There are many others that discourage buyers. What do you need to change? Identify aspects to change as you read through the book, using the tick boxes in the exit strategy 'to do' list on page 62 to help.

Identifying your SWOTS

SWOTs are the Strengths, Weaknesses, Opportunities and Threats within your company.

Your company review as you undertake this exercise should be revealing your SWOTs. Look at your company from an outsider's point of view and be absolutely self critical.

	Read about	Begin introduction	In progress	Completed
Company corporate structure	☐	☐	☐	☐
Company management structure	☐	☐	☐	☐
Develop Executive Team (your successor)	☐	☐	☐	☐
Organisation of financial structure	☐	☐	☐	☐
Introduce management accounts	☐	☐	☐	☐
Introduce budgets, sales targets and forecasts	☐	☐	☐	☐
Develop sales methods, marketing strategies and brands	☐	☐	☐	☐
Regular Executive Team meetings	☐	☐	☐	☐
Intellectual assets	☐	☐	☐	☐
Commercial matters	☐	☐	☐	☐
Business activities logistics and supply chain	☐	☐	☐	☐
Employee matters	☐	☐	☐	☐
Information technology	☐	☐	☐	☐
Reputation	☐	☐	☐	☐

Pre-sale activities

	Read about	Begin introduction	In progress	Completed
Due diligence	☐	☐	☐	☐
The sale process	☐	☐	☐	
After completion	☐			

Other activities to do

(This will be your own list of activities particularly pertinent to your own business.)

- Where you identify strengths, you should devise schemes and plans to position and develop them to give maximum impact.

- You should eliminate or work to improve all weaknesses that you find. Implement one or more urgent plans to address these negative factors.

- Opportunities will be around you all the time. You should learn to recognise them, and be brave enough to explore, and possibly take advantage of whatever new chances these openings give you.

- There will always be threats to your business. They can be financial or competitor threats. Keep a watchful eye, and be ready to act swiftly to counteract all threats. It is probably worth having a 'Plan B' at the back of your mind, just in case.

Preparing your customised exit strategy

- This is for your eyes only, and comprises your 'to do' list.

- Tick off and date all items on your list as they are completed. These lists may just be jottings by hand within your personal and private management accounts folder. That's OK. Any one casually glancing through would probably not understand your hieroglyphics, so confidentiality is preserved.

- Being a blueprint for action, you will find much adjustment and reconciliation will be necessary, between targets achieved or missed, your exit timetable and your exit strategy.

- Check out progress regularly and adjust, or do whatever is necessary to catch up.

◆ Despite adaptations, rearrangements and fine tuning, the overall programme will present you with a proactive route to your ultimate goal.

> Remain single minded and totally focused in carrying out this plan, which will probably take some years to finalise.
> This is your own, customised exit strategy.
> **The author can testify to the fact that this technique works.**

> Throughout the time leading up to exit
> keep pushing the sales and profit.
> Never let up on this.

Taking your time

Take your time to work out your best and most realistic exit strategy. What can be achieved, and in what time? Employees take the lead from you. For your plan to work you must be positive, motivating and hard working as an example to all. Lead from the front.

> Your next step is to set about the practical introduction of changes and modifications in order to remove all obstacles to a sale, to make the company attractive to a wide range of suitors, and reinforce buyers' confidence enough to progress to a sale completion.

> This is the most exciting time of your life.
> Sadly you must keep the enjoyment to yourself.
> You can do it. So go to it.

CHAPTER FOUR

Adopt a Corporate Constitution

In this chapter:

- *The importance of a company's constitution*
- *Types of corporate structure*
- *Executive roles and duties of private company executives explained*

The importance of a company's constitution

As you expand your company you will become aware that the business world sees companies that have a formal corporate constitution as being more professional and presenting less of a risk than a sole trader business.

You will notice that:

- Setting up a corporate structure with its associated legal duties and responsibilities, plus significant set up costs, indicates to everyone that your business is 'proper' and serious, not here today gone tomorrow.

- With a corporate constitution it becomes easier to obtain loans for expansion, because it is perceived that your company is run by several people who are prepared to take responsibility and be accountable for its results.

- To outsiders, a feeling of security is engendered that may influence the terms of loans or trade credit you take up during these times of growth.

◆ Coming towards your exit, prospective acquirers/investors will examine closely your corporate structure.

◆ There are situations when your company structure will affect the P/E ratio and buyers' willingness to proceed with negotiations.

> Legislative changes were made in 2006 and 2008 to the Companies Act, regulating corporate structure. Further changes are in the pipeline. It is therefore wise to check out and keep abreast of current compliance.

> Adopting a corporate constitution portrays stability and success, and subconsciously impacts on your customers, suppliers and employees, feeding through to the P/E ratio. Your company's headed notepaper and other literature proclaiming the company 'make-up' will proudly announce your professionalism which will hold immeasurable benefits.
> **You should formalise the company structure early in the company evolution.**

Types of corporate structure

Sole trader

A sole trader is a person who is responsible, on their own, for the running of a business, even though he may employ people to help out. That is to say, the sole trader alone makes all decisions. Generally, these businesses are small in turnover, since this is the way many companies start up. A sole trader business is usually unincorporated.

When the business grows, it may require financial support from banks or other backers. Inevitably this will require a different basis of company structure, i.e. partnership, or incorporated company.

Generally speaking, the status of sole trader is less prestigious than an incorporated limited company.

> As a sole trader you are personally responsible for all financial liabilities, which is what makes lenders uneasy.

Partnerships

This describes a business owned and controlled by two or more people. Partnerships hold less formality than a company structure with its requirement for formal registration and administration.

◆ There can be many pitfalls to partnerships. For instance, each partner **is held responsible** for the others' actions and decisions, even though they may not be involved in actually making and implementing those decisions.

◆ In partnerships there is no limit to liability, financial or otherwise.

◆ The partners are entitled to share equally in the capital and profits unless a **partnership agreement** has been legally drawn up to override the Partnership Act of 1890.

◆ A **partnership agreement** should be drawn up by your corporate lawyers, stating the following:
  (a) Exact details of the amount of capital invested by each partner.
  (b) In depth details of salary payments, profit allocation, company bank details plus cheque book access (how many, and who may sign cheques).
  (c) Exact division of working responsibilities, and time off.
  (d) Exact decisions regarding, illness, incapacity or death of each partner.

(e) The notice a partner must give before withdrawal of his interests.

(f) Decisions regarding remaining partner(s) buying the shares of a leaving partner.

(g) Decisions on whether a leaving party can sell his shares outside the company.

(h) In the event of a sale of the business, details of sales receipts apportionment between partners.

(i) Disputes procedure.

(j) Decisions on the treatment of goodwill following the departure of a partner.

(k) Similar decisions on the treatment of capital distribution upon departure of a partner.

(l) Decisions on the existence or otherwise of a non-compete clause following the departure of a partner, especially in event of a partner seeking employment elsewhere.

> For a partnership to work successfully, it is advisable that an appropriate written **legal partnership agreement** is in place from the outset.

In the matter of a company sale all partners need to be in total agreement with one another on all matters. Indeed, the success or failure of the business depends greatly on the harmony of the partners. This will be severely tested at the time of selling the business or as the partnership edges towards the exit of one or both partners.

> Disunity may destroy the chance of a company sale proceeding to completion. Partnerships can become especially vulnerable if the partners are a married couple. Marital (in)stability may affect the business partnership, and vice versa. This aspect should be given realistic consideration by each partner individually.

If your business is set up as a partnership, any acquirer will want to know the details of the partnership agreement beforehand, to ensure that he is not taking on trouble. He wants to know that he is buying the company complete, and that the person handling the sale speaks for all parties.

Partnership types

There are five partnership types:

1. Equity partners who contribute capital, and who share in the profits and losses.

2. Salaried partners who *do* receive a salary, but who may *not* contribute capital.

3. Sleeping partners, who may contribute capital and may receive a salary, but who *do not* take part in running the business.

4. Limited partners, where the liability of one or more of the partners is limited to the amount of capital they invest. This type of partnership requires registration at Companies House.

5. Limited liability partnerships (LLP) where the business, not the partners, has legal liability to third parties. This type of partnership also requires registration at Companies House.

> If your company is a partnership ensure at a very early stage that a legally drawn up partnership agreement is in place.
> This is what a buyer will expect to see.

Lawyers will advise whether it would be safer and more appropriate to set up the company as an incorporated private company from the outset.

A private company

A private company is made up of its shareholders, a company secretary who administers all regulatory matters, plus a board of directors who decide the strategic direction of the company.

The shareholders, by way of their ownership of the company's shares, actually **own** the company, collectively.

If you decide to set up a private company you would need to undertake a process known as 'incorporation'. This comprises establishing both a Memorandum of Association plus Articles of Association, which create the company's constitution.

Memorandum of Association

The Memorandum of Association is a legal document registered with Companies House containing company name, registered office address, location(s) of the business and its activities, together with details of its share capital. Lawyers will be involved in completing this process since company law will need to be precisely adhered to.

Articles of Association

Once again, this is a Companies House legal document, which enlists the shareholders, outlines voting rights, the conduct of shareholders, the conduct of directors' meetings, and the powers of management of the company. The composition of the Articles is fairly precise in format adhering to company law for its construction. The completed document is available for public viewing at Companies House.

Your lawyers' advice is crucial in formulating a company incorporation.

The board of directors (of a private company)

The board of directors have executive responsibility to **run** the company. Directors make policy and strategy decisions about the direction and manner of company trading, its financial affairs, borrowings and business expansion.

Shareholders

Shareholders are people who, having purchased company shares, have become its investors. They will play no active part in the day-to-day running of the business, or decision making on trading matters, company expansion, or even borrowing matters. They leave all of this to the board of directors. But they can expect to receive dividends proportionate to their shareholding, as a return on their investment.

The chairman

Being the most senior officer of the company, he leads the board of directors.

The managing director or chief executive officer (CEO)

His role is to drive the company's business activities forward towards achievement of budgets and targets set by the board.

In the case of small to medium enterprises (SMEs) it is often found that the chairman, and/or the managing director, is also the holder of the majority of shares. Hence the title 'owner manager', which appears frequently in this book. Corporate advisers often refer to him as the 'principal'.

> The role of each of the executives of the company is described later in this chapter.

Share ownership . . . classes of shares

Within any private company there may be several types (classes) of shares, each with different rights. There will also be a number of shareholders with different percentages of share ownership. It is sensible for you as owner manager to know who owns what, in what percentage, and to be aware of the voting rights of each shareholder in case of disagreements.

Loan stock (debentures) or preference shares

If a company borrows significantly large sums of money, to be repaid over a long period, the creditors may secure their loan by holding 'loan stock/debentures'. This is a form of legal stake in a company, whereby the creditors can have a say in company affairs without actually owning a piece of it. The interest on the loan due to creditors is paid ahead of the ordinary shareholders' dividend, and is irrespective of whether the company is in profit or loss.

Providers of such loans may be private equity companies such as venture capitalists, angels or other private investors. You should view them as 'senior shareholders' with rights ahead of ordinary shareholders. Their consent has to be obtained for a company disposal (sale). In the event of this happening, they would receive their share of the sale proceeds before distribution to the other shareholders.

Ordinary shares

In companies of SME size, the majority of shares are 'ordinary' shares, held by members (another name for shareholders) with different sizes of shareholding. At the time of disposal, these ordinary shareholders will receive a percentage of the sale proceeds, proportionate to their percentage shareholding.

Holders of ordinary shares

When the time for sale arrives it is essential that all members (shareholders) are willing to sell their shares, to the same bidder, and that all accept the same deal put before them. Disunity or unwillingness by any party to sell could wreck the deal, or at the very least delay proceedings and probably reduce the price offered.

You could encounter problems with minority shareholders who have little financial dependency on the company. On rare occasions it has been known for such minority shareholders, recognising that they are needed to approve a pending company sale, to demand a higher price for their own shares, or else they will veto the sale. Acquirers would rarely go along with this, and such suggestions could jeopardise the deal. Get to know your shareholders well in advance of a proposed sale, and forestall this type of occurrence. One answer is to anticipate such activity well before sale time by buying up their shares yourself at today's agreed prices.

> A long time before a company sale is given any consideration, it is sensible and practical to introduce a **shareholder agreement**. Strangely enough, some companies do not see this as important. But if everyone's interests are to be protected and properly served it is hard to justify this omission.

Things can move very fast at some points of sales negotiations and your advisers will consult only with you, the principal, not a committee of shareholders. So you must ensure that your decisions treat all shareholders equally fairly. This may be hard to do, without these earlier consultations that you made when drawing up the shareholder agreement.

Shareholder agreements

The shareholder agreement is a legal document drawn up by your solicitors. It is designed to give fair play to all members. There are some important clauses which should figure in the document especially as you approach sale time, in particular the 'drag along' clause and the 'tag along' clause.

'Drag along' clause

This will come into effect when the majority shareholder has received an attractive offer for the company, thereby producing a valuation for the company shares. In this scenario if the majority shareholder wishes to sell his shares, together with the rest of the company as a whole, he will need to serve upon the other shareholders this 'drag along' notice. The 'drag along' notice requires fellow shareholders to sell their shares to the same bidder. In effect, this means that the majority shareholder cannot be blocked by shareholders with fewer shares and voting rights.

'Tag along' clause

This would be used in the case of any person who owns more than 50% shares with voting rights, being induced to sell **his shares alone** to an acquirer. That is to say the acquirer is not going to buy the shares of any other shareholders. Any such sale would leave the remaining shareholders with shares that are without value and without power because the acquirer has more than 50% voting rights, and thus total control.

The 'tag along' clause entitles the minority shareholders to block the sale of those majority shares, unless the shares of the minority shareholders are included in the deal at the same price and terms.

In straightforward terms this protects the minority shareholders from being left with worthless shares.

Pre-emption rights clause

This clause seeks to establish pre-emption rights for existing shareholders, by introducing 'first refusal'. That is, shareholders wishing to capitalise their investment by selling their shares must offer them first to fellow shareholders, who shall have first priority, at agreed prices.

Only in the event that fellow shareholders do not wish to purchase these shares can they be offered outside the company.

Pre-emption rights are currently a topic of legal controversy in the UK, so discussion with lawyers is essential.

New shareholders

You would be wise to build into your shareholder agreement a clause that 'new shareholders must accept the terms of the existing shareholder agreements'.

Dealing with shareholders

> From the above information you can see that you should notify fellow shareholders of your intention to sell up as soon as you have received a firm offer that you feel is worthy of consideration.

However, it could be a big mistake to reveal to your shareholders **too early** that you are hoping to sell up or exit for these reasons:

- It would be natural for **shareholders who are also directors** to become concerned about continuity of their employment.

- This worry could result in them leaving the company, whilst still retaining their shares.

- Disaffected shareholders could reject outright any offers to sell the company.

- Shareholders may feel a better deal could be achieved, or feel the timing is wrong or the purchaser disliked.

- A shareholder could feel insecure about the future buyers, and refuse to sell his shares.

- A shareholder (with a chip on his shoulder) could pretend to be in agreement, whilst he attempts to sabotage the deal. This would be easily achieved by a shareholding director with executive responsibility and access to company information. In discussion with the Due Diligence auditors, or purchaser's representative, it would be a simple matter for them to present a picture that differs from actual fact, thus raising all manner of suspicions.

> In order to prevent sabotage of your exit plans, ensure that *you* filter all Due Diligence information that 'the other side' may need. When meetings between your company and purchasers are scheduled, allow your professional advisers to represent you, so that dissenters are excluded from any contact with buyers.

Preparing your shareholders for a company sale

See 'Director service contracts', Chapter 4, page 84.

It is far better that you should prepare the ground with your shareholders than announce suddenly 'out of the blue' that you have received an offer for the business. Hints at how well the company is doing, and 'a sale being possible, eventually, to the benefit of all', can begin to set the scene. But timing is everything. Don't discuss too early with your shareholders the detail of your exit strategy.

You should anticipate the safety or otherwise of your shareholding directors' jobs. Address this a long time before sale by creating director service contracts.

Shareholders who are *not directors* will naturally be compensated anyway by receiving a share of the sale proceeds, proportionate to their % shareholding. If your shareholding is more than 50%, ensure that you are able to 'control' your shareholders, and that they have confidence in you.

> **You** should endeavour to overcome all shareholder objections well before sale time. Check out the feelings of the shareholders' spouses and deal with those similarly. Do not fall out. Tact is crucial and persuasive arguments may win you the day. Repeating an earlier statement, **shareholder unity is crucial to a successful sale**.

Executive roles and duties of private company executives explained

Chairman

In any company the chairman's role is to 'lead the board'. He may be a non-executive director appointed by your financial backers, who employ him to protect and develop their investment. Or he may own shares in the company. In all cases he should have a service contract. His duties are wide ranging.

◆ He runs the board of directors.

- He chairs board meetings, seeing that they are held as frequently as necessary to facilitate the business of the company.

- He has strong powers to insist that there is a balance of knowledge and experience in the membership of the board of directors, so that every sector of the company is represented.

- He ensures that each board member, executives and non-executives alike, play an active part in running and controlling the company and have a say in matters under discussion at board meetings.

- He must verify that all important and significant matters are on the agenda and that each board member is briefed in timely fashion, so that they may make a knowledgeable contribution.

- He should ensure that all board members are fully discharging their fiduciary duties and responsibilities as directors.

- He is required to 'stand back' from the company, taking an overview, thus ensuring obligations to the shareholders are being fulfilled and that the board is complying with codes of best practice in corporate governance.

- It has become quite fashionable for the chairman to be the spokesperson for the company in matters of publicity, although this is not a mandatory role within his position.

Managing director or chief executive officer (CEO)

In many SME companies, the owner manager, or principal, acts as the managing director, because he has the greatest shareholding. In other companies the managing director may have **no** shares. However, as the 'senior director', the **managing director** has an important function.

- It is his duty to direct the company activities to ensure that the investors' funds are safeguarded.

- He should endeavour as far possible to bring the company into a profitable status.

- He is answerable for trading results plus the whole gamut of company activity in all its forms. 'The buck stops here.'

- He holds the authority to oversee development of strategy and attainment of goals. In doing this he will consult with all directors, but especially those with executive function.

- He is obliged to ensure company compliance with all governmental regulations, keeping within company law.

- He is responsible for driving, motivating and inspiring executive directors to achieve the targets set at board meetings.

- He will work closely with the chairman.

Any acquirer/investor will check out the owner manager/MD closely via professional associations and networking, as they look for honesty and straightforwardness in his reputation. Any hint of past dishonesty may reflect badly on a company sale.

Acquirers/investors would generally prefer to see a secondary or Executive Team reporting to the MD and running the company's everyday affairs rather than an MD who 'runs the show himself'. Thus, when the sale occurs, the MD can walk away, leaving the Executive Team to manage the company, having all the 'know how' necessary to do so.

See 'Develop your own successor... make yourself redundant', Chapter 5.

Executive directors who own shares

See 'Director service contracts' this chapter, page 84.

These are directors, working in the company, who *are* shareholders, and thus will benefit from the company sale proceeds, at the time of disposal, directly proportionate to their shareholding. However, their future employment within the 'new' company may not be assured.

They will certainly be vulnerable because:

◆ New owners may not wish to employ them, or even keep them in the same job.

◆ They may also lose their rights to certain company perks.

If you devise director service contracts, these directors can be given some protection. However, do not tie them in for **excessive** compensatory payments or notice since this could jeopardise your deal.

Executive directors *without* shareholding (DWS)

These are directors, working within the company, but they *do not hold shares*.

> DWS is one of the thorny topics of a company sale, needing careful deliberation well in advance. If handled badly, the sale itself could be compromised, or sales proceeds considerably reduced.

It is the shareholders who have the main say on 'if, how and when' the company is sold. Some of the shareholders may well be on the **board of directors.** And since it is the board of directors that make policy and strategy decisions these directors would expect to be involved in the decisions surrounding the proposed company sale. Any director who is a shareholder will receive part of the sales proceeds.

But directors who **are not** shareholders (that is, executive directors without shareholding, DWS) **will not** usually receive any rewards as a result of a company sale, so have no incentive to support such a sale. Indeed, they could find their job endangered because the purchaser: does not like them; would be duplicating staff; or has other plans.

If you inform these DWS too far in advance that it is your intention to sell the company you may create risks of these dangers:

♦ Sensing the insecurity of their job, DWS could leave suddenly, which at such a busy and sensitive time would be difficult, because of the Due Diligence examination to come (see Due Diligence, Chapter 16). To any potential purchaser, losing someone who is probably a member of the key personnel does not send good messages about the company, and at worst could give cause for such apprehension that acquirers/investors withdraw all offers.

♦ There is danger of the DWS gossiping, resulting in loss of staff and loss of an acquirer.

♦ If DWS are not told about your decision to sell, until after the sale has been completed (and DWS have in effect been 'sold' to the purchaser, as part of the deal), the new owners could encounter difficulties because of animosity from these same

DWS. This would be understandable, since they would normally be expected to be involved in 'senior' decisions regarding the company.

◆ This resentment could cause problems with client accounts, suppliers and other day-to-day management of the company's trading activities.

◆ In such an instance, there is a risk of you being penalised by not receiving your full sale proceeds, held over in escrow accounts (see Sale process, Chapter 15). At worst you could receive claims for damage, from the buyers.

◆ Where DWS discover that negotiations are in progress (without having been informed) the danger exists of the purchaser via Due Diligence auditors being given incorrect information, which could have dire results.

Suggested solution

Make a declaration to all DWS collectively of your intention to sell the company, just as you are about to enter discussions with interested parties. Negotiate a deal with these 'directors without shareholding'. Make it financially worth their while to support the sale, and stay on as employees/ directors afterwards, if required to do so by the new owners. Remember all directors need to be 'on side' if a deal is to be concluded satisfactorily.

We suggest that you offer incentives to them, which they would receive contingent upon the sale proceeding to completion. A suggested figure would be one year's salary, or X% of the sale proceeds shared between them all. Very large sums should not be offered, since DWS would then have sufficient funds to leave the company immediately post sale, which is not in anyone's interest and could lead to the buyer raiding the escrow account, thus reducing the sale proceeds.

The subject of DWS is of considerable significance, and should be an early discussion with corporate advisers. The outcome of these decisions could have far-reaching implications. At worst, the deal could be abandoned.

> When you finally decide that the time is right to reveal your hand, give consideration to the spouses of your DWS. They can be very influential in driving their 'other halves' in just the direction that you don't want. Perhaps you should undertake a round of dinners or social gatherings, where spouses are present, to 'test the water', and even guide things along your chosen path.

Non-executive directors (independent directors)

These are directors who do not work within the company. Their position on your board is to act as an adviser to the company. However, they are held to be legally responsible for the company activities in just the same way that executive or working directors are, because they are in possession of the company confidential information.

- Non-executive directors (NEDs) will usually have or have had a successful business career elsewhere. Their role is to remain independent of the board (indeed they are often referred to as 'independent directors').

- Their experience allows them to make impartial judgements on the company's performance, on company business matters and to comment accordingly.

- They can offer impartial business advice.

- They can introduce contacts, to assist towards the company's growth, financial stability and success.

◆ They can act as a private sounding board for the managing
director, so that he may obtain an unbiased objective opinion
of any schemes under review.

> If you reveal **too soon** to NEDs your plans for company sale, there
> should not be too big a problem. This presumes they can be trusted
> to be discreet.

If you don't yet have any NEDs you could consider the
appointment of these aides, because their experience can often be
invaluable. They are frequently insisted upon by private equity or
other financial supporters. Their terms of contract are usually
short, which may coincide with your own exit plan. They should
receive service contracts similar to those of directors. NEDs'
external contacts can often be useful when prospective purchasers
are being sought.

Director service contracts
This is a normal contract of employment, detailing:

◆ The precise nature and hours of the work.

◆ Any restrictions imposed upon them.

◆ Remuneration details, commissions, incentive schemes, sick
leave restrictions, precise car provision (type, size), expense
allowance and all other such particulars.

◆ Details regarding termination of employment, i.e. number of
weeks' notice, salary entitlement in lieu of notice, and whether
the company car may be retained during notice, etc.

These are sensible clauses in their own right, but if read at the time of an impending sale, they should allow for the eventuality that the new owner may not employ these directors in any capacity at all, post sale.

> In devising 'protective' clauses for directors, you should be aware that purchasers will fully evaluate them at the Due Diligence examination. Should they prove too restrictive, or expensive, the deal could be reduced in value or fall down completely.

You should take the advice offered by your experienced corporate lawyers and your corporate finance specialist in the compilation of these contracts.

Company secretary

In many companies of SME size, the company secretary is also a director. Other firms may have a company secretary who holds the title, but fulfils another role entirely as his main function. Yet the post of company secretary is significant in all companies.

◆ The company secretary is responsible for keeping statutory registers.

◆ He must complete and send to various authorities statutory returns at regular intervals.

◆ His knowledge of your company's commercial matters will be essential during the sale and purchase process.

◆ The importance of his position requires that he should be treated as though he holds director status, reporting directly to **you.**

The next chapter moves on away from the corporate structure of the company to explain the role of the management structure of the company.

CHAPTER FIVE

Introduce a Management Structure into Your Business

In this chapter:

♦ *The employee management structure*

♦ *Develop your own successor... make yourself redundant*

♦ *Risk factors in developing one individual successor*

♦ *Who should be in the Executive Team?*

♦ *Developing the Executive Team*

♦ *Benefits of an Executive Team*

♦ *Executive Team meetings*

The employee management structure

Your company will benefit by having a formal management structure. This should define a work unit, together with its manager, and the reporting lines of people within the work unit. Example: sales consultant reports to the sales manager, who in turn reports to the sales director, who reports to the managing director. It should be possible to present this management structure as a chart enabling you to visualise the whole organisation.

See Management structure chart, page 88.

This management structure is motivating for employees, illustrating a career path that individuals could follow. As part of this format it is recommended that each person holds a position that has a proper job title (i.e. credit control clerk).

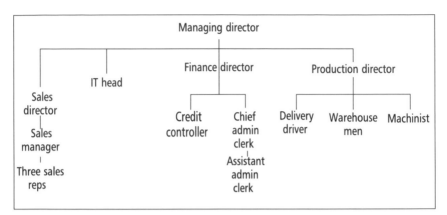

Figure 3. Management structure flow chart.

A clearly defined management structure will positively influence the P/E ratio.

Benefits to the company of an employee management structure

◆ Improved efficiency overall because of an orderly organised work structure.

◆ Reliance for everyday matters on the owner manager is reduced.

◆ Company risk factors are reduced because there is more than one decision maker.

◆ Financial institutions will approve of efficient management structures.

◆ **Post sale** the company can still be run efficiently by its managers.

◆ It gives a professional appearance to your company and broadens the range of interested investors/acquirers.

◆ P/E ratio will be improved.

Advantages to employees of an employee management structure

◆ It is easy to introduce staff incentive schemes.

◆ It's also easy to introduce performance targets.

◆ Your staff gain motivational 'career paths'.

◆ Training needs in your staff are easily identified.

◆ Less chaos all round... Well motivated happy and loyal staff.

The result is tight company control.

> When introducing a management structure you will only achieve real success if the actual management positions have their precise objectives and purpose described accurately. It is important that managers should receive training in both man management skills as well as training in the job itself. For instance, a sales manager should receive training in both managing a team and how to achieve sales.

Develop your own successor...make yourself redundant

Your role is significant in the running of your company. You are its driving force; you have the business acumen, knowledge of the products, the markets, the costings and the politics.

Yet it is a weakness for a company to be reliant on one person.

Is there someone else within the company with all that expertise, initiative and enterprise? Probably not!

> If you have no obvious successor, prospective buyers could think that the company will fold without your influence. Thus it is of major importance to find others who can do all that you do. In other words, replace yourself.

This will take some time. Developing a successor entails the selection of someone who is:

◆ financially capable;

◆ strong in management skills;

◆ a good sales person;

◆ knowledgeable about other companies' activities and your company's marketplaces;

◆ knowledgeable about your product/service range;

◆ knowledgeable about supplies, suppliers and competitors;

◆ well known and respected in your industry;

◆ well regarded by financial institutions;

◆ as ambitious and energetic as you are.

If there is already someone that fits that picture then you should develop a training programme for them, within their current role.

Training your successor requires them to:

◆ accompany you to appointments;

◆ get to know how you think;

◆ get to know how you would act in any given circumstance;

◆ become privy to company secrets;

◆ become a clone of you.

At that stage they should be given responsibility and opportunity to test their new skills.

Risk factors in developing one individual successor

It is certainly essential to develop your own replacement, even as a safety factor in case of illness. But to put all the effort into one individual carries risk.

◆ Suppose they are lured away by a competitor. This would be dangerous since they know all of your company's confidential matters.

◆ Suppose they are unable to continue in your company employment through illness or personal circumstance. You will have wasted all that development time, yet still have no successor.

◆ Unwittingly, you may be training someone to bid for a management buy out (MBO).

◆ You could be training someone to set themselves up in competition to you.

You should build an Executive Team to replace yourself.

Who should be in the Executive Team?

You are seeking people who will act as a team to replace *you*.

Every company will be different in how it constructs its management, but the selection of staff to fulfil the Executive Team positions is not difficult, as they are probably involved in the tasks already. Indeed, many may already hold director posts within your company.

There should be a representative of each major function within the company. Suggestions include:

- head of sales and marketing;

- head of finance and commercial matters;

- head of production;

- head of IT.

These people will be **key personnel** within the company.

Developing the Executive Team

Your staff will find that managing at executive level can be daunting. The new senior responsibility it carries takes time to perfect.

Your Executive Team must learn:

- to personally accept responsibility and accountability;

- the skills of managing the company as well as managing their 'section';

- the use of management accounts to decide courses of action for your company, as well as their own division;

- how to direct and manage staff.

You need to encourage them to make their own decisions, without reference to you.

In the early days of Executive Team development some decisions that they make will be bad ones. As a trainer you should accept that this will be the case. Making a good, or 'the right', decision is an art to be learnt by the team.

Benefits of an Executive Team

+ Buyers can see that the company does not rely solely on you. This obviously reduces the risk factors and would reflect positively in the P/E ratio.

+ Gradually, as the team becomes proficient, the role of running the company will have devolved to them, leaving you free. You can take holidays or be ill in peace!

+ Training and delegation of duties is motivational for all staff involved, and leads to a harmonious working environment. Acquirers/investors will look for this in their preliminary 'under cover' visits to the company.

+ During the period of sale negotiations the company can keep running smoothly and normally, supervised and directed by the Executive Team, allowing you time to confer with corporate advisers.

+ Post sale, the company can still run efficiently even without you. This is your objective. Your P/E ratio will benefit.

+ Buyers could readily introduce their own managers to lead the Executive Team, thereby introducing the focus and ethos of the new owners.

> **Warning**
> It is wise to delegate to a team of successors the everyday affairs of the company. But do not **abdicate** your responsibilities. Ensure that everyone is behaving honourably and properly. You are still fully responsible. People who do abdicate often find that their business fails.

Executive Team meetings

Your Executive Team need to appreciate the value in managing company affairs using regular monthly meetings where they can:

◆ Analyse monthly management accounts.

◆ Check progress on targets, for all sections.

◆ Check progress on all budgets.

◆ Reset objectives where necessary, taking action as needed.

◆ Discuss issues needing close attention and tight focus.

You should attend these meetings yourself, using them as an opportunity to train your executives in the arts of directing and controlling the company efficiently. When the staff are competent, it is wise to allow them to take turns in chairing the meeting.

> Purchasers will evaluate the Executive Team's decision-making strengths and make judgements on their cohesion as a working unit. A strong team may well tip the balance in favour of acquisition of your company.

Your next step is to firmly prepare the financial status of the company in readiness for the company sale.

CHAPTER SIX

Organise Your Company's Finances

In this chapter:

- *What first attracts a buyer?*
- *Prospective buyers will probe these aspects*
- *Financial integrity and good reputation*
- *Introduce a financial infrastructure early on*
- *Your company's profit*
- *A closer look at your gross profit*
- *Net profit*
- *Management accounts*
- *Finance at the growth stage of the company*
- *Grow your order book as an asset*
- *Financial view of organic growth*
- *Financial view of growth by acquisition*
- *Financial view of growth by franchise*
- *Borrowing for growth*
- *Things you should be aware of in applying for a loan*
- *Buyers' view of 'borrowings'*
- *Financial activity just before the company sale*

What first attracts a buyer?

You will not be surprised to hear that it is your company's financial standing that is often an early interest for an acquirer/ investor (although this is not the only reason buyers may be interested in your company). Before making an approach to you

they will have obtained copies of your accounts from Companies
House and conducted a preliminary financial appraisal.

Their attention will centre on:

- Latest company annual turnover £££;

- Annual turnover for each of the preceding three years;

- Net profit % and net profit £££;

- Gross profit % and gross profit £££.

If the buyer likes the above information enough to proceed
further, he will approach your company requesting more 'in
depth' data. He will be looking for:

- Financial advantage to be gained from this acquisition;

- Opportunity for profit and growth;

- Low risk investment opportunity;

- Synergies with *his* current business(es).

Having signed a confidentiality agreement via your corporate
finance specialist he will go on to probe your company finances in
some depth via the Due Diligence process.

> You should familiarise yourself with the Due Diligence process. Be aware of its
> critical importance to any company sale. See Chapter 16.

Prospective buyers will probe these aspects

£ Your **last three years' internal management accounts** matching these with your audited accounts. Buyers will interrogate the financial integrity of your data preferring your management accounts in the format of spreadsheets and reports taken straight from your computer system.

See 'Financial infrastructure', page 100.

This professionalism has a positive effect on the P/E ratio.

£ Your preceding three years' **annual turnover** will often be appealing to purchasers if a sustained year-on-year growth has been attained. Erratic turnover spikes or one off/occasional successes raises suspicion that this is not a reliable and safe investment prospect.

A steady upwardly climbing year-on-year annual turnover is preferred. Steady growth will have positive influence on P/E ratio.

£ Your company **profit** from the three preceding years will be scrutinised, and will form an important part of the company valuation when negotiating the sale price of the business. **Company valuations that use an average of the last three preceding years' figures may not always be in your best interest**.

Consultation is advised with your auditing accountants, and corporate financiers, when preparing 'pre-sale' trading results in order to present accounts in the most advantageous way.

Your profit has dramatic impact on P/E ratio.

£ **Your management accounts showing budget forecasts** of earlier years will be compared with actual results achieved in those earlier years. Variances will require explanation. Judgements will be

See Appendix 'Setting a budget'.

made on your forecasting skills. A track record of poor forecasting may cast doubts on the company's future projected figures contained in your Information Memorandum, making them seem suspect. Thus the deal could be jeopardised because the buyer senses risk, believing the forecasts may be wild guesses.

> You should always endeavour to set annual budgets and targets that stretch the company towards growth, but nevertheless are achievable.

Gain approval of Pension Regulator to ensure compliance and eliminate problems after the sale.

£ Your company pension scheme *must* hold adequate funds to meet all obligations to past and present employees especially where the pensions are final salary schemes. If there is **inadequate funding** the deal **will be off**.

See 'Credit Control Management', page 102.

£ Your company's efficiency in managing the credit you grant to your customers will have considerable impact on your company's ability to grow and remain solvent. It is said that poor credit control is the major single reason for SME company closures.

At the Due Diligence examination the credit that you routinely grant to customers will be evaluated via the age of debt report, alongside its estimated recovery time. The P/E ratio will be adversely influenced if the outstanding debtor figure is high and the estimated time of recovery long. Your company's bad debt policy is important to your cash flow, and management of your finances.

Introduce strong credit control systems plus even stronger bad debt policies to have positive influence on the P/E ratio. Check out your 'age of debt' regularly.

£ Your company's depreciation policy should be realistic and sensible. Due Diligence will require full explanation and corroborative data in items of significant value. These figures could well be important in company sale price negotiations.

See 'Due Diligence', Chapter 16.

£ Goodwill in your balance sheet will always be regarded with suspicion. It is better written off by yourselves during the pre-sale period, since it will have negative impact on the negotiations anyway.

See Glossary for explanation of goodwill.

Goodwill is a subject that can raise heated arguments because the buyer will have to write it off, either immediately following acquisition, or over a period of years post acquisition, thus denting the value of his purchase. Consultation with your auditing accountants on this matter is essential since there are accounting rules governing the way goodwill may be treated.

Take accountant's advice on treatment of goodwill in your books.

Comprehensive management accounts are the guide to successful cost recognition. See Appendix 'Management accounts explained'.

£ To enable you to run your company finances efficiently enough to produce real profit, all costs will have been taken into account. These must all be identified in your monthly management accounts.

True cost recognition is the key to successful pricing of goods.

Buyers like to see

◆ Tight financial control, led by a professional head of finance using computer records, spreadsheets, reports and management accounts to support his financial control.

◆ Budgetary forecasts for the current full trading year, together with trading forecasts and budgets for the future.

◆ Costs identified and taken into account when setting pricing policies.

> Credible financial planning plus maintenance of tight budgetary and financial controls will be influential in attaining a high P/E ratio.

Financial integrity and good reputation

Many a deal has failed because the owner manager's reputation for straightforwardness was in doubt. Any facts considered doubtful in the financial information given to purchasers creates a suspicion of risk for the buyer, which could kill the deal.

Introduce a financial infrastructure early on

Keeping your records straight

Accountants will always advise you to be precise in your record- and book-keeping. Accurate accounting processes will aid financial success. Without doubt, the more profit is made the less is the risk of a company failure.

> Poor book-keeping can be misleading, and monies previously thought to be profit may not in reality be so.

Introduce IT accountancy software

As your company grows, the complications in 'balancing your company's books' can be readily overcome by use of a suitable customised computer program.

◆ Successful company growth is dependent on use of accurate information.

◆ Developing forecasts and budgets becomes easier when using computer-generated information. Many a company has faced failure by basing projections on inaccurate information.

◆ Training of managers, especially the Executive Team, becomes easier with the aid of spreadsheets and reports.

◆ Acquirers/investors feel a level of confidence in data generated by reputable computer software.

◆ Development of your **exit strategy,** intertwined with your **exit timetable**, becomes a manageable task with help of computer reports.

P/E ratio will benefit.

Selecting your head of finance

When you select your head of finance we suggest you seek someone with, at the very least, the qualification of 'management accountant'. Management accountancy is exactly as its name describes: preparation, recording and interpretation of financial information, suitable for managing the company's finances. This is quite adequate for your company, where the strategic planning is probably carried out by you, the owner manager.

It is quite feasible that a well incentivised and successful management accountant could make the grade to your company financial controller or financial director. To achieve such status he will need to be a decisive decision maker, who will take full responsibility for the financial decisions that he is involved in.

The character, financial competence and integrity of your financial head will be covertly judged by the acquirers/investors representatives during Due Diligence. His honesty and reliability will positively affect the credibility of your company's fact and figures.

Credit control management

Your company will only be as healthy as its cash flow.

See Appendix, 'Cash Flow Forecast'.

♦ Cash flow is strongly influenced by the speed with which customers pay invoices.

♦ Prolonged intervals before payment is received may deplete your company's resources, thus calling for financial assistance from the bank or others. Should your forward cash flow report reveal that this is likely you should take speedy advice from your auditing accountant before the company is forced into closure.

See Appendix, 'Age of debt'.

♦ Preparation of a monthly cash flow report will show the highs and lows of cash at bank, allowing you to plan outgoing expenditure. It will alert you to cash shortfalls ahead. Buyers will wish to see this report at Due Diligence.

◆ Incentivise your credit control clerks to achieve specific 'age of debt' collection targets. Well-motivated credit control clerks, who get to know your customers' purchase ledger clerks, can often obtain earlier receipt of payments. By getting to know your customers' payment procedures, your 'age of debt' can be reduced.

◆ If you discover that credit control is your company's weak spot you should investigate

> Investigate factoring services.

factoring. There are companies and banks who offer factoring services as a means of controlling your outstanding credit. In these schemes your outstanding debt is 'bought' from you, leaving the factoring company to chase the debt themselves.

Meanwhile, your company has received outstanding payment from your clients minus the % charged for the factoring service. The advantage of this system is that your cash (minus charges) is where you want it...collected and in your bank.

> Buyers acknowledge the benefits of outsourcing the credit control function as a means of financial control.

◆ You are advised to introduce a definite credit control policy as a means of dealing with bad payers. When your policy is decided upon this should be computerised. The issue of invoices, statements of account, warning letters and court action letters can be automated, giving reliability. Your company's credit control policy and bad debt write-offs will be scrutinised at the Due Diligence examination.

◆ You would be wise to initiate a standard policy of checking out a prospective client's credit worthiness. Why take on bad risks?

- Similarly, a regular check should be kept on major **suppliers** via their credit ratings. Bankruptcy of a major supplier can cause untold difficulties to your ability to actually deliver your products/services and could lead to a major interruption to your cash flow and business operation.

- It is possible to evaluate credit worthiness on-line via credit reference agencies, so checking up is quick and easy.

P/E ratio may be influenced by adverse customer credit issues. If the risk factors are high the deal could be abandoned

Your company's profit

As your company generates its profit so you increase the value of your company. Acquirers/investors will scrutinise what you do with your profit.

- You could use it to make loan repayments.

- You could take it as your salary payment.

- You could use it to pay dividends to shareholders.

- You could use it to accomplish a mixture of the above points.

- You could re-invest it into the company to fund growth or become a cash asset (cash at bank)

- Cash at bank (in saving deposit not working capital) will influence your company valuation in a very positive way.

> Your profit is a major factor in valuing your business and plays a significant part in an acquirer's/investor's decision to purchase, invest or otherwise.

Your auditing accountants will declare profit in the accounts every year that you make profit.

> Company profit is taxable. Unwise owner managers attempt to make **no profit** so that they pay **no company tax**. They spend 'the profit' on additional salaries, equipment, marketing, etc. Thus they avoid tax. This approach is not likely to bring buyers flocking to your door.

Acquirers/investors will be looking to see how much profit was made in preceding years and to see if there is opportunity for 'add backs'.

See 'Add backs', page 49.

To be really keen on buying into your enterprise buyers want to see a steady, **sustained profit growth** over these past years.

Next, they want to see your **steadily rising revenue and profit stream** predicted into the future.

> In the years before exit, invest in audited accounts filed at Companies House. Make efforts to achieve profit each year. Taxes will be due on this profit. But this will stimulate the interest of prospective buyers. This is where high P/E ratios lie.

A closer look at your gross profit

You will know that gross profit is the difference solely between the selling price of your goods/services and the buying price of all the components that make up the goods/services.

Example

100 widgets are sold for	£4,000
Purchase price of 100 widgets, paint, repackaging material, labels and delivery charge, total	£2,500
Producing a gross profit of	**£1,500**
In this case the gross profit margin % is 37.5% of the selling price. For the purpose of this example VAT has been ignored.	

As you see the gross profit makes no allowance for the overheads of your company, such as salaries, rent, heating, lighting and so on.

Buyers' view of gross profit

Gross profit margins of 50% or higher of the sales figures indicates that the supply chain purchasing is being accomplished professionally, and good prices are being achieved for its products/ services. This demonstrates desirable gross profit.

Gross profit margins of 30% and lower indicates that purchasing costs are only average (could do better). Your selling prices are perhaps too low also.

Gross profit margins are often dictated by your business type. Typically, computer software has high profit margins; distribution is much lower.

Net profit

Net profit is arrived at by taking the gross profit margin calculations and then further deducting a figure for overheads.

(Overheads include all salaries, premises costs, etc, as seen in your management accounts.)

Example from above:

100 widgets are sold for	£4,000
100 widgets plus paint, repackaging material, labels and delivery charge are bought for	£2,500
Gross profit made	**£1,500**
Deduct overheads costs say	£1,100
Net profit	**£400**

In this case net profit is 10% of the overall sales figure of £4,000 (again VAT has been ignored).

Buyers' view of net profit

Acquirers will be looking for a net profit of 10% or more if possible.

◆ Buyers who are looking to purchase, then run your company as it stands, will want the net profit figure and percentage to be as high as possible, and sustainable. Thus they can quickly recover money spent on acquiring your company and make profit for themselves.

◆ If the net profit is less than 10% then it may seem to acquirers that either:
 1. the total overheads are too high and not under control; or
 2. the selling price of goods/services is not consistently high enough; or
 3. not enough is being sold.

◆ **An acquirer** may feel that your company could benefit financially by using his own management team, who will achieve more competitive buying prices, reduced overheads and higher sales.

◆ **An investor** will use your company net profit to re-invest in company growth, then later sell on your business, thereby capitalising on the company's increased valuation.

But low gross or net profit figures will have a negative impact on the P/E ratio.

> **Action to take**
> During your pre-sale phase drastically reduce overheads to give enhanced net profit. This will give opportunities to positively influence the P/E ratio. See Pre-sale activities, Chapter 14.

Management accounts

Your management accounts, calculated and presented to you as spreadsheets on a monthly basis, will undoubtedly form the most important tool in steering the company through its growth and on to exit.

◆ Ensure that all sections of your company are represented so that a complete picture of the company unfolds monthly.

◆ Check out these accounts so that nasty surprises do not await you in the future. Use with a monthly prepared balance sheet and profit and loss account, together with a cash flow forecast for best results.

◆ Accurate costings for each and every department, and activity, reported in your management accounts should produce the

See Appendix, 'Management accounts spreadsheets'.

basis for price setting, market selection and steering of the company towards success rather than failure.

Finance at the growth stage of the company

Growth is vital

A company whose turnover remains static will soon wither and die.
But you should be aware that **sudden** growth can bring with it
some financial stresses. To be most effective both at the time you
are growing the business and later when you have reached the exit
stage, your rate of growth and chosen marketplaces is impressive
if it can be seen to belong to a planned expansion programme as
demonstrated in your budget forecasts.

Top line or bottom line growth?

This is a fairly regular question that will arise for you.

♦ Should you be proactively seeking to gain lots of turnover, by
  bulk selling of items and selling cheap? The 'pile them high
  and sell them' cheap philosophy.

♦ Or should you be aiming to sell fewer items at higher prices
  each, thus producing higher gross profit margins?

♦ Or can you achieve a mixture of both methods?

This is not a debate for this book. It will depend on the financial
circumstances of your company, your sales abilities, your
marketplace, and the speed with which you wish to grow your
company.

This question is one which will keep recurring, almost annually as
you press forward with growth. Your management accounts will
define your way forward.

However, it is worth knowing that it is no good 'working for nothing' or 'being a busy fool' by producing a big turnover with no net profit.

> It is the net profit that will interest acquirers/investors and drive a high P/E ratio.

But by building up volume sales to clients, it is possible to negotiate with suppliers, so that you pay lower prices for the supplies. These lower prices increase your gross profit margin. So, a mixture of marketplaces and differing 'selling out' prices for the same product is a good way to grow rapidly.

CASE STUDY

One SME company traded by selling its 'own brand' toilet tissue, complete with special 'own brand' dispenser that eliminated waste of toilet paper. It contracted to sell the dispensers to hospitals, together with the toilet paper itself, in large quantities. To achieve this it purchased the toilet tissue by bulk buying from suppliers at huge discounts.

To the other customers, who numbered a lot of clients in the small business sector, a lot of retail outlets, a lot of offices, etc, the same 'own brand' toilet tissue products were sold at much higher prices.

Thus, the business satisfactorily grew at a reasonably fast pace, achieving good gross profit, good net profit, and marketplace control with its unique dispenser range.

The contracts, giving marketplace control in a broad range of different market segments, produced an enviable future order book, which proved to be a valuable asset at the owner's exit.

Grow your order book as an asset

Growing your turnover drives your profit, and interests acquirers/investors.

If your company is a small consultancy selling knowledge/technical 'know how' as its product range (for instance, a computer consultancy) and there are only one or two people within the company with the 'know how', then it will prove difficult to grow.

Because there are too few people to support your customers, you will be strangled by your inability to produce more than a modest turnover. This may be a good sound business but will always be small. The exit here will be by way of closing down, because there are no assets, and no future order book to pass on. The product range is the owner's expertise.

CASE STUDY

One small computer consultancy expanded by writing and developing their own software programs. These became their own intellectual property, assets in themselves. Their business grew by licensing their software to customers. They contracted to support it, using 'own trained' technicians. High level of profit was produced because they have no competitors. Thus they created a valuable business with IT intellectual property as assets, plus assets in forward order contracts, together with unique products, producing high profit margins.

With some thought everyone can grow their forward order book.

Many companies choose to grow their order books:

◆ by contracts with their clients;

◆ or by market place control;

◆ or niche products.

Review your business, analysing suitable methods for you to grow the business. Do you want slow growth by organic methods, fast growth by acquisition, or wide geographical coverage by franchised growth?

Financial view of organic growth

An organic growth programme, delivering gradual expansion, budgeted for and financially well controlled, is not likely to cause financial problems.

◆ Tight credit control and rigorous cash flow monitoring are the key to expansion. Your sales people should give warning of looming possible sales order explosions, to avoid cash flow difficulties.

◆ It is a sudden, very large order, contract or big sales opportunity needing considerable additional expenditure to fulfil the order that could overstretch your financial resources.

◆ Whenever sudden growth requires large capital expenditure, a cash shortfall could be created. So it may be necessary to borrow additional expansion capital.

See 'Borrowing for growth', page 114.

> Consultation with your auditing accountants is essential if cash shortfalls are likely.

Financial view of growth by acquisition

The impact of expansion by acquisition is very quick and very sudden growth, with high associated costs.

◆ If growth is to take place via acquisition (of another company) then it is pretty certain that borrowing will be necessary. Use your team of auditing accountants and corporate lawyers in raising funds and completing negotiations. Then confirm that financial controls are very quickly established. This is a dangerous time, when a company could easily over-reach itself.

◆ Acquisition often means borrowing from private equity or business angels, who will want the security of equity in your company, with pre-set terms and conditions, in return for a capital loan.

◆ Acquisition requires you to be certain that what you buy is worthwhile. Sometimes 'buying in turnover' can be a mistake. As soon as you have bought the company their customers could transfer their orders elsewhere. Assess this risk in consultation with your corporate advisers. Be sure to cover this danger via access to the seller's escrow account (your corporate lawyers will advise).

◆ Merging two companies following acquisition can be fraught with difficulty and cost. There will be differing systems of operation, and financial control. This will need speedy resolution, before chaos ensues.

◆ Be sure you have covered all the risks.

Financial view of growth by franchise

Franchise can produce a network of operations identical to your main site, enabling quick geographical coverage.

◆ If you are going to run a successful franchise chain it is essential that the parent company (probably your main site) is trading successfully, as a role model.

◆ Supporting your franchisee will require you helping them to achieve 'look-alike' systems, premises, equipment, stationery and your 'brand identified' products. Clearly the cost of this will be greater in some set-ups than others.

◆ Much of this set-up cost can be recovered by an initial down payment made to you from the franchisee.

◆ Where a franchisee builds a profitable business, your company can probably claim a share of this profit under the terms of the contract between your two companies.

> You may be required to give ongoing support with marketing activities to find customers for the franchisee. This can be expensive, but is a cost to be shared between the franchisor and the franchisee.

Franchising can be a successful way of quickly building turnover and profit. But it is not the easy option, and does require a cash outlay from you first. There could be pitfalls. So consult your financial advisers with your business plan, before seeking growth capital from investors and going ahead with such a project.

> Franchising associations should be consulted. Research this expansion move carefully before commitments are made.

Borrowing for growth

It is quite commonplace for businesses to require additional capital for expansion. So who to approach and how to go about it? Fortunately the Internet is quite helpful.

Lenders

Banks

Because your own bank knows you best you should approach them before trying any others, when applying for a loan or overdraft facilities. Security of the loan is their prime concern, plus your ability to repay. Their loans are often straightforward interest-bearing repayment loans, complete with repayment schedules, enabling you to plan repayment timetables, essential for the exit plan.

Grants

There are many different types of grants around. Explore this, as many are industry or geographically sensitive. Grants are generally straightforward repayment loans, but with some restrictive clauses and covenants. Check whether/how the grant restrictions will impact on your exit strategy.

Business expansion schemes (BES)

These are similar to grants, and again often industry sensitive, with restrictive covenants. But there are many BESs around, often linked to the EU. The Internet plus your local Business Links office are helpful. So too are the CBI, the IOD, the Federation of Small Businesses, and your trade organisations.

Private equity

These are venture capital companies or business angels.

This type of investment loan will frequently require some equity from you, in the form of shareholding in your company plus an interest-bearing repayment schedule. Because they have become a shareholder in your company they will also take dividend payments, plus compensatory dividends in particular circumstances. Check out these compensatory payments, because they could deplete your profit and your ability to grow your 'cash at bank'. The private equity company will generally wish to appoint someone onto your board, often in a non-executive role (director or chairman usually). This person is there to safeguard the interest of the investor.

> **Repaying private equity**
> In the event of your company being sold to totally new owners at the company sale, your private equity backers will receive a share of the sales receipts from the sale proceeds, proportionate to their shareholding and in accordance with your company Articles of Association. Your exit plan should take account of this.

> Prior to any company sale taking place, it is important to check out and be compliant with the terms of agreement that you made with your private equity company. Their percentage shareholding is usually sufficient for them to take a view on your plans for the company's disposal. You will need to discuss your proposals with them before the sale. New acquirers/investors will be unlikely to assume any of your company's loans when they purchase it.

Things you should be aware of in applying for a loan

◆ As principal, you yourself must be totally involved in the application. Indeed, judgements will be made on the project itself, on your ability to carry it through and on your business acumen.

◆ You must be absolutely clear in your own mind exactly how much you require.

◆ You should also be absolutely clear what the loan is to be used for. Perhaps it is working capital, or for equipment, machinery, or even additional staff salaries. Define this precisely, prior to application, since full explanations in writing will be required.

◆ If the requirement for financial support has been triggered by a big contract opportunity, you should get the loan approved by the lenders *before* signing this contract (there could be all manner of difficulties if the loan is refused).

◆ A formal business plan, complete with cash flow forecast should accompany your loan application. This should also lay out the features and benefits of the product range, an explanation of the targeted sales marketplace, and the price structure(s) of the products/services you offer.

◆ Accompanying the business plan should be copies of your last year's audited accounts plus your management accounts and budgets from the past, demonstrating that you are reaching your forecasted targets.

◆ From the information you present (as spreadsheets), the precise usage of your loan should be clearly explained. A proposed repayment schedule, worked out by you, should also appear. In preparing this information you are demonstrating that the loan is to be used as predicted, and not just frittered away.

◆ Your information pack will be presented to a 'loan committee' by your contact with the lenders. Your contact's recommendation will be used to decide the outcome of your request. It is a wise move to motivate your contact to speak in your favour to the panel, before the application is presented.

Criteria used by lenders when awarding funds

A good product and company can be ruined by a poor manager. A poor product or company can be a soaring success with a good strong manager.

This is the yardstick that lenders use to make decisions when granting loans.

Judgements are made on 'the principal' – that is you

- Are you a good strong manager, easy to get on with, straightforward and honest?

- Do you know the product range, marketplace and competition really well?

- Will you drive forward the project to success as predicted in the business plan?

- Are you a 'yes man', weak and easily influenced by others? Or do you strongly know your own mind?

- Lenders are very obviously keen to gauge risk, so a professionally presented business plan addressing the issue of risk management (what if things go wrong?) will impress them.

- Lenders will be looking for a return on their investment (ROI). In other words, 'What's in it for them?'

Successful loans

These must appear in the balance sheets and all accounts.

Buyers' view of 'borrowings'

Providing loans are correctly displayed in the company audited accounts, and there are no prohibitive clauses attached to the loan, they only figure as part of the sales negotiations. You, as owner manager, will repay any outstanding loans on sale completion. Loans will not be assumed by acquirers/investors.

Financial activity just before the company sale

This is probably the most important phase in your exit.

Using your auditing accountants' expertise, your annual accounts should be presented in a fashion that is attractive to acquirers/investors.

By reading the 'Pre-sale activities' in Chapter 14 your accountants can make the necessary adjustments to your balance sheets and accounts that will improve your exit sale opportunities.

CHAPTER SEVEN

Construct the Company Growth by Sales and Marketing

In this chapter:

- *Your annual sales turnover*
- *Review your company sales*
- *Get on with it*
- *What acquirers/investors want to see in your company sales turnover*
- *Your sales approach is a vital ingredient*
- *The importance of progressively rising sales*
- *Gaining progressively rising sales*
- *Has your sales turnover plateaued?*
- *Diversifying*
- *Your company's customer base*
- *Growing your company sales*
- *Contracts with customers*
- *Marketing*
- *Branding*
- *Brand recognition*
- *Further marketing activities*

Your annual sales turnover

At start up and for some time afterwards your sales seem to come from anywhere and everywhere.

After a while, your management accounts indicate that you should grow more quickly, create more profit, deliver closer to home or some other factors. And thus you go about achieving these goals.

> **Be warned:**
> As soon as you have decided that you are going to sell the company, you need to change the focus of the business. So, you should begin with a company review.

Review your company sales

- ◆ What are the company strengths and weaknesses, opportunities, threats?

- ◆ Checkout the product/ services range
  - Have you got any new intellectual assets (Chapter 8) worth developing and bringing to market?
  - Does your current product/service range have unique features that you can develop and promote?
  - What is the best way of bringing these promotions to customers? (Brochures, product training for staff, adverts, exhibitions, mail shots and so on.)

- ◆ Check out your existing and prospective marketplaces:
  - Can you develop within the market segments you currently supply? (How? What's needed to do so?)
  - Can you specialise in other market sectors? Identify them precisely.
  - Which marketplaces will impress acquirers/investors?
  - Which market segments are growing or in decline?
  - How can you go about reaching these prospective clients? (Tenders, mail shots, telesales, field sales force, etc.)
  - Are there any special requirements your company should have before approaching these prospects? (Accreditations, specialised training in client needs, etc.)

◆ What time span have you got? Your exit timetable will identify this.

◆ Time is important because you need to identify whether quick growth is needed or slower organic growth. (Acquisition, organic, bulk sales, tenders or franchise.)

◆ Check out the economic climate. Business is cyclical with business downturn occurring every ten years or so. Check this out with your bank's economic adviser.

◆ Choose products and markets that will survive a global business downturn and live on to the upturn in the cycle.

◆ Cast your net wide, with lots of clients and, if possible, more than one market segment.

Get on with it

Make the decisions on sales direction as early in the company evolution as possible. **Then go for it**. Do not deviate, or slow the pace.

> It is your determination to achieve whatever exit goals that you have set regarding time, turnover and profit that must now drive you and the company forth with single mindedness, vigour and energy. You will find that you become ruthless in your determination to succeed. A triumphant exit depends upon your being totally focused.

Remember you will need to show prospective buyers three years' audited accounts prior to exit, depicting good turnover and profit. So you must begin now. **There is no time to lose.**

What acquirers/investors want to see in your company sales turnover

◆ Strong sales turnover figures around the time of exit, having shown steady growth in the preceding three years.

◆ Lots of opportunity for future growth. Buyers may be impressed if your future order book is full. They can see what sales turnover awaits them.

◆ Loyal customers developed in particular market sectors.

◆ Blue chip customers are a bonus, giving your company certain kudos.

◆ Acquirers/investors may have been seeking the opportunity to trade with 'blue chips' and not yet found the way to do so. Buying your company would give them the access they need.

◆ A large number of clients, who order regularly.

> A large customer base is valuable to buyers.

◆ Contracts to supply customers, running on into the future and expiring at different times, is further proof of future revenue stream.

◆ Companies in declining or uncertain markets may still be of interest to some buyers. But the valuations used and sale proceeds from the deal will produce low P/E ratios. This will be seen as 'acquisition that needs some help', maybe even a 'fire sale'. Very strong warranties and guarantees will need to be given as part of the deal.

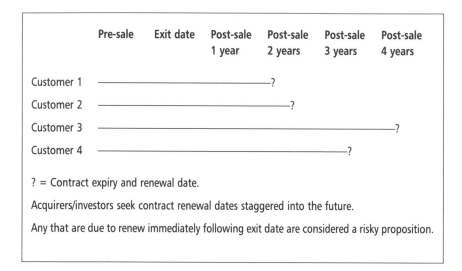

Figure 4. Acquirers seek contracts running into the future
and not all ending at the same time.

Your sales approach is a vital ingredient

Are you passive or proactive?

You should give thought to your company's approach to
obtaining sales orders. It tends to be either passive or proactive.
Which type are you?

The passive sales ethos

> Passive sales companies risk the company withering, then dying.

◆ This describes the company that is content to
let things roll along, allowing trade to 'come
to them'.

◆ Not much financial reward will be earned by
a passive enterprise, where the sales are hoped for rather than
created.

- In 'passive ethos' companies it is difficult to plan upwardly rising growth patterns.

A low P/E ratio will be attained by this lazy type of approach.

The proactive sales ethos

- This describes dynamic and powerful sales strategies conducted with drive and energy.

See 'Growing your sales' in this chapter, page 130.

- Marketplaces are researched and contacted with vigour.

- If success is not forthcoming from one market sector, another is swiftly approached.

- The plus points of the product range are enthusiastically demonstrated to clients.

- This vitality, being infectious, engenders client confidence and sales ensue.

- Proactive companies are less likely to suffer recessionary problems because new markets are continuously tested, and converted into customers.

See 'Check out your market-places', page 121.

- In an economic downturn, proactive sales forces will still be actively seeking business, looking for the opportunities that will always be there for energetic companies.

The proactive ethos will always be led by you

Your energy is 'caught' by the Executive Team, then spread throughout the company, producing rising turnover year on year. It will not be the easy option for you. Keeping on the pressure at all times is tiring, but it is also fun and rewarding to watch company growth.

P/E ratio will benefit from proactive sales ethos.

The importance of progressively rising sales

Purchasers like reassurance that the future holds a smooth growth potential, without peaks and troughs. Steadily rising growth patterns from the preceding years will give buyers some confidence that growth is possible.

This diagram shows steady annual year-on-year increasing turnover.

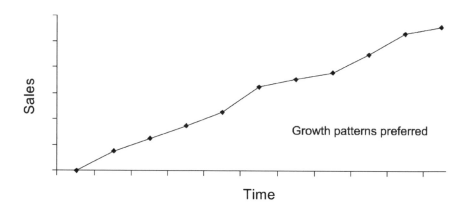

Figure 5. Steadily increasing sales patterns preferred.

To gain progressively rising sales turnover year on year:

Sell more products/services overall
Achieve more sales transactions
Find more marketplaces
Approach more prospective clients
Sell to more clients
Retain all existing clients
Encourage each client to increase his spend
Increase the client unit sales value at each order
Introduce additional products to each client
Revive dead or dying accounts
Replace dead accounts with actively spending accounts
Each year increase turnover above the rate of inflation

Year on year

♦ Each year's sales turnover must increase over last year's results, **at a rate higher than the country's rate of inflation** at least (or the company has not grown but just remained static).

♦ Buyers dislike a static, flat performance.

♦ Buyers dislike erratic spikes of success followed by troughs of nil or low sales. This is too risky. They cannot be certain of any future trade, and would have spent the acquisition money all for nothing.

♦ Achieving this reliable sales pattern requires development of **a company image** that encourages customer loyalty, and will survive a company sale.

A history of steady sales growth is an important feature of negotiation.

> Acquirers may well have borrowed to complete the acquisition of your business. The repayments of this loan will be made from the profits that they make from your business.

Has your sales turnover plateaued?

This can happen if the product/service has reached a peak of popularity, or the marketplace has disappeared.

CASE STUDY

The ashtray market. This was a booming industry, until smoking was banned in public places. Ergo far, far fewer ashtrays needed.

A flat or plateaued turnover will not excite buyers, and would command a low P/E ratio.

Diversifying

Examine your company closely. There are often opportunities for diversification if sales stall.

◆ If the British marketplace is challenged, what about export to foreign countries?

◆ If customers are dwindling in your chosen marketplace, select another industry or two to develop. Perhaps the product range may need tweaking to achieve this.

◆ If all else fails, look for different products/services to add to your range, to take over from your original product.

◆ Perhaps you just need to analyse your product and markets to ensure that, for the foreseeable future, your product range and marketplaces are stable. This would impact positively on the P/E ratio.

Take a proactive view to be progressive and successful.

> **Beware**
> A business whose sales turnover is stagnating will not be at all interesting to any buyer. You will find it difficult to sell up.

Your company's customer base

You should regularly examine your customer base. How many **active** customers do you have? What market segments are you strong in? How do you approach new clients? Are your clients reliable in re-ordering and paying you? Are they reducing their spend with you? Why? Customised computer reports will make analysis an easy task.

Acquirers/investors like to see that your customer base contains a **large number** of actively ordering clients. Inevitably, Pareto's rule will apply, in that 80% of your business will be with 20% of your clients, as it is with all businesses.

If it is possible to build your trade by specialising in a certain market segment this would put the company into a strong position for an acquirer wishing to enter that trading sector.

Buyer interest will be stronger if you can build a representation in more than one market segment. This avoids risk if there should be a downturn of business in that sector.

Your customer base will be closely scrutinised at Due Diligence. Client numbers, names, frequency of ordering, order values, etc, will be requested, especially the top 20 or so clients.

Growing your company sales

Achieving progressively rising sales turnover comes down to these main methods: growth by acquisition, organic sales growth, or franchise.

Growth by acquisition

Benefits

- Growth by acquisition can quickly increase your turnover (and probably profit), enabling you to rapidly reach company readiness for exit.

- By purchasing complete companies you can rapidly increase your customer base.

- Acquisition can bring in a big turnover increase at a stroke.

> But you should consider what you are trying to gain from the purchase. Is it just company turnover, or are there other features that will be useful to your growth? View the list below.

- Will you gain prestigious clientele?

- Will you gain company expertise, and know how?

- Will you gain substantial profit?

- Will you gain strength or entry into particular market sector(s)?

- Are there synergies with your current business?

- What do you stand to gain in actuality?

- Other benefits?

Dangers in acquisition
- There is risk in the acquired clients' loyalty. Will they transfer to you, or will they go elsewhere?

- Is the promised turnover actually sustainable over the period that it takes to pay for the acquisition?

- Will you have to borrow substantially to complete the purchase?

- Will these borrowings transfer to your balance sheet smoothly alongside the assets that you have purchased?

- Does the acquisition give your company a stronger balance sheet, or have your borrowings weakened your position? Are you too highly geared?

- Search out any previously unforeseen risk and danger.

Following the acquisition there are many practical considerations.

- How can you merge and run the two companies?

- Can profitability be improved by divestment of property, assets, or surplus staff?

- Can profitability be improved by bulk buying of supplies?

Many companies have found that growth by acquisition is a step to quick growth. But it can be risky. Seek professional advice *first*.

Growth by acquisition is not for the fainthearted.
But it can produce increased company sales turnover fairly quickly.

Organic sales growth

Using organic sales methods it may take a long time to reach the exit turnover you need. However, it is usually fairly safe and the company develops many skills along the way.

Organic growth describes selling your products/ services using your chosen sales methods of a field sales force, internet, retail, mail order, telephone sales, etc. or a mixture of all methods, supported by marketing programme(s). Using organic sales methods, company turnover should be driven to rise by a regular percentage each year, always above the national rate of inflation.

Creating organic sales

Your product range and customer type may dictate sales method.

There are many ways of reaching potential customers. The best results may be found from a mixture of methods. Sometimes, the product range dictates the best way forward. Sometimes the chosen marketplaces dictate method.

Field sales force

A field sales force is very expensive, needing cars and promotional material support.

This describes proactive visits by your sales staff, to potential clients. Their objective is to win sales orders, and to advertise your company's presence in the marketplace. To be successful the representatives must be well trained, well presented and highly motivated.

Field representation carries the high associated costs of travel expenses and cars. Careful consideration should be given to representatives' remuneration. To be cost effective an element of financial reward linked to successful sales results is to be recommended.

> Link financial reward to successful sales results.

Perhaps you could introduce a generous commission system? All field sales staff should work to achieve individual sales targets, by which they are closely monitored. You would be wise to insist that retention of their perks, and even the job itself, should be contingent on targets being met, monthly/annually.

> Give sales reps incentive to achieve their targets.

Your field sales staff need monitoring, possibly by **field sales manager(s),** who by the nature of their work will be an expensive overhead. You can mitigate this by linking **team success** to field sales managers' remuneration.

> Reward field sales managers via *team* results.

Telephone sales

When run as an in-house section (rather than outsourced), telephone selling can be a very cost effective sales system. It can be proactive, by 'cold calling', which describes outbound calls to find new customers and create orders.

Telesales is particularly cost effective where the product lines are goods or services needed repeatedly by customers. Using telesales staff to take repeat orders is far more economical than using field sales staff visits. Where repeat order clients are computer monitored you can ensure that your company receives these orders rather than the competitors.

Nowadays, sophisticated telephone and computer technology allows telesales operators to **draw up contracts** for provision of products or services, once again precluding the need for expensive field sales representation.

Telemarketing

You could use telemarketing to support your marketing activities. This describes proactively following up exhibition leads, sales promotions, advertising campaigns, or appointment setting for field sales representatives.

It can also be reactively taking inbound calls relating to mail order clients, promotions, exhibitions, etc.

Telephone sales and telemarketing need a telesales manager to maintain standards and targets.

Mail order sales

Distribution of sales catalogues or literature to prospective clients is necessary, but when strengthened by 'telesales follow-up', excellent results can be achieved.

Online sales

You will have seen the growth in books, clothing, tools, equipment, food, etc. traded online. The world has found it enjoys the ease and benefits of online shopping. And many a company has discovered that they owe their continuity in business to online trade. The immediacy of online ordering appeals to many customers.

However, this method of selling can lead to those unwelcome spikes of unpredictability.

Overcome online unpredictability with reliable orders that can be foreseen and forecasted. Develop schemes that tie customers into your company with regular trade commitments, but using the online facility to top up their orders.

> A mixture of contract and computer diary programs, plus telesales, gives proactive forward planning.

CASE STUDY

A stationery business supplier contracts with his customer to become his sole supplier of stationery, whereby the customer uses the online facility to place actual orders as required. Quite quickly a pattern of the customer's regular needs can be monitored, allowing prediction of forward sales orders. This allows a programme of reminders to the customer by phone or email. This is proactive selling with a vengeance.

Retail sales

You will notice that retail shops belong to the passive ethos, where the company 'waits for clients'. So to increase sales turnover, a pro-active programme of luring customers to the store with advertising, brand promotion, special offers, etc is essential.

> Retail outlets depend on sufficient customers. Position the shop well. Count the footfall. Advertising, brand promotion, and good reputation are essential.

Company reputation is important too. Customers need to know that they will get value for money.

Attracting sufficient clients is the way to succeed in retail.

The **growth** of retail trade will frequently mean expanding the chain of outlets (as well as selling more in each shop).

Using an online ordering system linked to a catalogue is also proving a popular addition to retail sales creation.

Retail is always in danger of producing spikes of successes, followed by troughs of sales shortfall. However, a smoother pattern of retail growth can be achieved if the expansion of business uses the **franchise system,** with your company as the 'home' or 'host' head office. (Consult British Franchise Association before taking this step.)

Expansion by franchise

You could consider franchising as a way of expanding your network of shops, or other types of outlet.

> The most succcessful franchises have a strong *brand* orientation.

Franchising your business enables a franchisee to run a store or another type of operation as a mirror of your 'home' branch, operating in its image. Franchisees purchase a licence from you to do so. The franchisee accepts terms that enable certain contracted revenues to be conveyed to the home branch. (See Figure 6.)

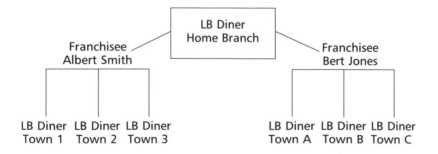

Figure 6. Retail franchise operation

Franchises are successful in all types of outlets nowadays, even solicitors, accountancy practices, and hotels. Considerable effort is required to set up and support a franchise, but the benefits of such a scheme to the franchisor (**you**) is increased trade plus client retention.

Franchise schemes benefit from the establishment of a strong brand identity that is easily recognised and well respected.

> Franchising is a popular and successful means of attaining growth. It is especially useful in extending your business geographically.

Contracts with customers

Advantage of written contracts with customers

- You are certain of receiving revenue from contracted customers, over the life of that contract, say three, five, seven or even ten years.

- Client retention is facilitated, thus trade is smoother, without peaks and troughs of turnover.

- You reduce competitor activity with that client.

- You can forecast ahead for both sales receipts and supply chain management.

- Knowing your future supply needs, you can make term, fixed price, contracts with **your suppliers** (benefiting your profits).

- By developing a bond with your contracted clients, you can work at increasing their annual spend with you.

Contract format

♦ Contracts can take the format of contracted agreements to supply, re-stock, service, deliver, maintain, to accommodate, treat, supply services in emergency, plus many other schemes.

♦ Similarly, contracts may take the form of rentals, leases, agreements, schemes.

♦ All contracts are agreements contingent upon you supplying goods/services, and the client paying you.

Products/services that seem difficult to 'contract'

Most products can be supplied on some kind of contract. But it may take some thought to attain this.

> For instance:
> Laying block paving driveways – having had his driveway paved a householder is unlikely to require this again.
> **But**
> Suppose the block paving company becomes a supplier to house builders/ local authorities? Opportunities are then created for contracts to supply and maintain all driveways, school paths, care homes paths, parks and all of their other properties on a regular basis.
> Or suppose the client is a retail park developer? This creates opportunities to lay and maintain car parks, walkways, etc on a regular basis and on contract with the retail park developer.

You may still feel uncertain about contracts. But if you consider the benefits of a constant revenue stream it may be worth a second look.

CASE STUDY

A flower shop reliant on passing trade.

First they joined a national florist distribution chain.

Then they set up their own chain and introduced champagne, chocolates and jewellery into their range.

Then they contracted to supply local hotels, shops, reception areas with weekly flower displays.

The business is stable and growing.

With thought, lots of things are possible.

Products unsuited to contracts

Ultimately, there will be some products unsuited to contractual arrangements. Designer clothes perhaps?

See 'Branding', page 142, and 'Brand names', page 150.

In such cases the creation of your sales turnover is dramatically enhanced if a 'brand name' has been built up, with a brilliant reputation. This will require strong marketing efforts to entice clients.

See 'Marketing', page 142.

Things you should know about contracts

If you have been awarded a contract this *does not necessarily* produce actual sales transactions and consequent sales revenue. In issuing contracts, government bodies, large industrial groups and others feel that they have accepted your company as an 'approved supplier'. It is then up to their local administrator in each individual establishment to actually select your company and then place the orders.

So, having won the contract, **your sales staff need to contact sites and sell your product/services**. Being an approved supplier makes this an easier task, which can often be accomplished via telesales.

Contract tender and renewal times are interesting stages. It is **not always** the cheapest offering that will win the day. They are usually judged on 'value for money', which may take in a variety of additional points for consideration. Where a contract has been running well, a rapport should have been built up between customer and supplier. So, at renewal time, the incumbent supplier often has an advantage.

Do not rely on this.

A professional competitor could break this conviviality by producing an additional benefit that the customer can't ignore.

Be canny.

> In general terms, contracts are a good thing. But towards the end of a long contract, the profitability of the business being transacted is open to question. You may be running the contract to give advantageous 'top line' sales figures, but time elapsing since the contract was awarded to you has seen an increase in production or delivery costs, such that the 'bottom line' or profit is challenged

When setting up the original contract, especially those having a duration in excess of one year, build into it clauses to counteract inflation.

Buyers' view of contracts

The predictability of a reliable revenue stream incoming to the company in future years is a definite plus, but contracts could hold dangers for the unwary.

+ A contract that is shortly to change following acquisition will be seen as a risk by acquirers, especially if the management or ownership is about to change. Customers could see change of ownership as a reason to re-tender the contract. Hence the risk factor. The acquirer could have 'bought' and paid for the contract as part of the deal, but end up without it if the tender process chooses another supplier.

◆ Contract clauses should hold no restrictions or caveats for new owners.

◆ Most contracts can not be assigned to another company. This means that you cannot 'sell' the contract itself to another company.

◆ To overcome this clause, the company as a whole can be sold. Thus the company and its contracted service remains the same. But it is owned by new people.

◆ There should be consultation with the customer, after the sale has taken place, introducing them in a cautious and respectful manner to the new owners of the company. This will allow the customer to question the new owner, and decide whether the contract may continue.

> Acquirers/investors do not want contracts that all end at once. The advantage of contracts is that they run on into the future past your exit date, expiring at different times to give the new owners a guaranteed revenue stream after they have bought the company.

Bear in mind your eventual acquirer when composing the terms of contracts. Contracts that become onerous or hold risk will deter acquirers/investors.

> When writing contracts you should build in these clauses:
>
> ◆ Allowance for inflation-beating price increases.
> ◆ Mid-term review of prices within the contract (can be useful).

Marketing

Marketing is the underlying platform of activity and planning that assists in creating sales orders.

> All marketing activities should be controlled, costed and evaluated individually as to their success in producing sales orders.

Marketing comprises decisions made on the appearance of the product/service range, promotional literature, the pricing structure, the words used to describe the goods, literature, mail out programmes, marketplaces tried out (market testing), branding matters, exhibitions, advertising programmes, product placement and so on. Combine all of this with customer categorisation and you have 'marketing'.

From this you may gather that marketing provides the framework to direct and support sales order taking. Larger companies run the marketing activities as a 'section' complete with section head, possibly a marketing director, manager and staff.

But SMEs just conduct the marketing activities as part of their sales programmes.

Branding

An important part of a company's marketing plan is branding.

◆ Customers come to **trust** a reputable brand name.

- Customers will **seek out** a memorable brand name.

- Branding identifies your company, setting you apart from other companies in a similar line of business.

- Branding can increase company turnover.

- Branding and good reputation are crucial to successful retail expansion.

- An identifiable brand is almost essential if growth is via franchising.

Benefits of developing a brand identity

- Acquirers/investors could be actively seeking a branded range to add to their portfolio.

- Acquirers/investors may wish to purchase 'the brand' in order to control its use.

- Having a branded product within your range may offer the opportunity for 'second tier sale'. This is where the brand name is purchased separately from the company itself, thus raising additional sales receipts for the vendor.

- Branding can be important where franchising is a chosen expansion option.

Brand recognition

A brand is actually an intangible item. It can't be seen and instantly identified as belonging to your company. The trick therefore in giving it an identity is to match your brand name to your logo, thus creating your trade mark.

See 'Brand names', page 150.

You should develop your brand early in the company's evolution. It will assist your company development, and if it is well enough established it will form an important part of sales negotiations.

All of the above give good reasons for a high P/E ratio.

Further marketing activity

Targeted exhibitions, although expensive and time consuming, can be an excellent way of finding clients, but may not always produce immediate sales revenue. However, exhibitions are a good way of promoting a brand and advertising your company's presence in an industry.

> The cost of exhibitions can be reduced if you suggest that **your suppliers** help to pay for your stand, displays and visual aids. After all, they too will benefit from your success.

Clientele categorisation is well recommended. By selecting your customers by type, perhaps their business activity, you can build up strengths in particular market segments. Analyse your customers, ensuring that your business is operating in rising market segments, rather than those which are becoming financially unviable or unpopular.

> **Customer categorising**
> Decide which marketplaces you wish to sell to.
> Obtain lists of these outlets.
> Further categorisation by postcode ensures deliveries close to each other, thus developing geographical clusters.

Product performance, suitability and lifecycle should be examined. Product adaptation or design change in order to excite customer interest should take place as early as possible.

Strategies should be developed to supply products/services 'on contracts', or maybe rental/lease schemes, to tie clients in to written long-term trading agreements.

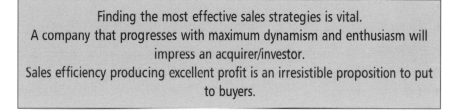

Finding the most effective sales strategies is vital.
A company that progresses with maximum dynamism and enthusiasm will impress an acquirer/investor.
Sales efficiency producing excellent profit is an irresistible proposition to put to buyers.

CHAPTER EIGHT

Recognise and Secure Your Intellectual Property and Assets

In this chapter:

♦ *What are intellectual property and assets?*

♦ *Have you got intellectual property and assets?*

♦ *Patents*

♦ *Trade marks*

♦ *Designs*

♦ *Brand names*

♦ *Copyright*

♦ *Domain names*

♦ *Protecting intellectual assets*

♦ *The value of intellectual assets as a tool to influence P/E ratio*

♦ *Identifying your company's intellectual assets*

♦ *Marketing your intellectual property and assets*

What are intellectual property and assets?

When you put the company up for sale, that's when intellectual assets and property really come into their own.

Indeed, the P/E ratio you would hope to obtain could be strongly influenced by any 'fully protected' intellectual assets owned by your company. In some cases the sale may hinge upon the assets themselves.

To be attractive to buyers, it is the level of protection that will be of significant interest. Registration ensures that the asset can't be copied or reproduced. The buyer is buying into uniqueness. Intellectual property is now registered at UK Intellectual Property Office (the new name for the old Patents Office) www.ipo.gov.uk.

Have you got intellectual property and assets?

Intellectual assets is a collective term used to describe all of the items of intellectual property possessed by a company. They are nowadays described as 'assets' because it is recognised that they hold a financial value.

Intellectual property describes resources inextricably and very closely linked to and owned solely by a company. Sometimes, the resources involved may be intangible items, such as names. Or they may be visible and thus tangible things that are the result of creativity, innovation or invention within the company.

In some companies these items of intellectual property have been conceived as the result of a research and development (R&D) programme. Others items of intellectual property could have resulted from 'ideas', possibly even a brainwave. Often they will be innovative adaptations to existing products aimed at improving effectiveness and efficiency. But in each case it is considered that the company is the owner of these assets, rather than the person who discovered them.

Business managers are nowadays learning to place value and importance on these assets and thus go to some lengths to give them protection.

> The UK Intellectual Property Office describes intellectual property as falling into four classes: patents, trade marks, designs, and copyright.

Patents

Patents are rights of protection that are given to cover inventions of products involved in the commercial and industrial world. Patents can only be granted to human inventions, not new scientific discoveries (such as a new law in science). Patents that are granted must be renewed every fifth year up to 20 years.

> The most important factor in gaining patents is that the new product or process has not been exhibited or shown to members of the public, until after the patent application has been filed. So keep it under wraps until the patent is granted.

A new system of patent that is under discussion currently is the Community Patent, to give protection throughout the EU. Its purpose is to replace the European Patent system. This would mean that a Community Patent on your product gives the product protection within all the countries signed up to the Community Patent. Currently, the patent system requires applicants to apply for separate patents in each of the countries where the product is to be available.

> If your intellectual property is to be influential in gaining a high P/E ratio or to be important in **attracting** buyers, the process of gaining a patent should be given serious consideration.

Trade marks

Trade marks cover any mark or sign that distinguishes the goods and services of one trader from those of another. A sign includes, for example, words, logos, pictures, or a combination of these. Basically, a trade mark is a badge of origin, used so that customers can recognise the product of a particular trader.

> There are specific rules as to what comprises an acceptable trade mark, upon which the UK Intellectual Property Office will offer guidance.

Trade marks are frequently linked to brands, since they make the 'intangible brand' into a 'tangible' format. For instance, the brand and ethos of McDonald's fast food chain is projected by the trade mark of an arched 'M', readily distinguishing it from other fast food outlets. By registering your trade mark you are in effect registering your brand or brand name.

Having a trade mark linked to your brand name has two distinct additional advantages.

◆ Firstly, in the matter of brand protection, where the name of the brand is the same as the name of the company. In such circumstances, if there is a trade mark to identify the brand, it is extremely unlikely that another company of the same name would select the same trade mark as your own. Thus 'passing off' is prevented.

◆ Secondly, a company operation, which has become easily identified by its form of branding (for example Burger King), offers the brand owner opportunities to franchise the operation as a whole, thus making good use of the 'brand ethos' and reputation. The company owning the brand could allow others use of the operation and brand name 'under licence'. This can be financially rewarding for the brand owner.

Designs

'**Design rights**' come about via the registration of the design of a product. Once again, this is an arrangement made in conjunction with the UK Intellectual Property Office whereby you register the appearance, either in whole or in part, of a product. Features taken into account are particular lines, contours, colours, shape, texture or materials of the product or its ornamentation.

> It is understood that:
> a registered design has to be new and not previously shown to members of the public. It must be sufficiently different from how a similarly concerned product would normally look.

The UK Intellectual Property Office says that designs fall into three categories:

1. **Registered design**, which gives protection lasting for 25 years.

2. **Design right**, a free automatic right. This gives protection for up to 15 years.

3. **Copyright** covering an artistic design, drawings or plans that is an automatic right if the design is not intended to be mass produced.

The UK Intellectual Property Office offer guidance on details of registration.

Brand names

Brand names are an important intellectual asset. They are the better known area of intellectual property. A brand name is the title by which we recognise a company or a product (for instance, 'Kit Kat').

Brand names are extremely valuable to their owners because they will be the word used specifically by customers when placing an order, thus ensuring sales of that specific product.

> Brand name(s) can be of great significance and value even though a brand or brand name is not actually tangible. Making your brand recognisable and a tangible item is achieved by creating logos, trade marks, colour themes, slogans, jingles, that are 'attached' to the brand in question. To work successfully the brand must be readily identifiable.

Alongside this, it is important that you develop a 'brand ethos', whereby you are known for the particular way in which your company operates. This would include your attitude to clients and suppliers, the quality of product/service offered to clients, durability of products, and all the good and special features of your product and your company that you wish to project to clients. To the observer this should all spell 'high standards'.

The ethos can be further conveyed at your offices with good and easy car parking for visitors, and a welcoming reception area. Don't forget the telephone, which is probably the first contact that clients make with your company. It should go without saying that your staff, without exception, should convey their belief in the brand, their enthusiasm for the company, and the chosen company image via their friendly, knowledgeable and helpful manner. Thus a prospective client will associate safety and a good experience with your brand name that now has seemed to him to have gained a tangible quality.

> In creating a brand image as described above, you have now turned your intellectual property into an intellectual asset.

Copyright

At present there is no official facility to register copyright.

◆ Copyright covers literary and artistic material, layouts for publication, music, films, sound recordings and broadcasts, including software and multimedia.

◆ The UK Intellectual Property Office advises that 'at the very moment the above material is written down, recorded, broadcast, etc the copyright is created'.

◆ Copyright on the original piece, together with the author's name, and date of its first writing, should be retained as proof of origination.

◆ Copyright does not apply to ideas, only to the way the author or artist has presented them.

Currently, copyright rules are under legislative scrutiny, and may well be subject to change.

Domain names

Domain names, that is your registered internet address(es), are becoming an especially important item of intellectual property, in this computer age, as online trading becomes ever more popular.

◆ Companies seek to register websites as a protection for their brand names.

◆ Registration should be accomplished at registration sites on the internet, taking advice wherever possible to avoid 'scam' registration sites.

◆ Much work is currently being done to increase the number of sites available for internet domain name registration by Internet Corporation for Assigned Names and Numbers (ICANN).

Currently the UK Intellectual Property Office remains aloof from domain names.

Protecting intellectual rights

Protection of your trade marks, design rights and patents is worthy of consideration as exit looms.

Some sceptics may doubt the value of the expenditure involved. But consider these facts.

◆ If another company uses 'your' company name, brand name, trade mark or logo, would this confuse your clients?

◆ Could it lead to loss of business? Suppose the 'thief' is not of good reputation, and thus your own company's reputation is jeopardised.

◆ Consider the consequences of your design or invention being copied and passed off as though it belongs to someone else?

These problems could prove financially damaging. And certainly at company sale time any confusion about the ownership of intellectual assets will be positively discouraging to any proposed acquirer.

> There are many benefits to safeguarding your significant intellectual assets by way of registration.

Advice can be obtained from independent specialist IP protection companies. They can be found via the Internet as well as the UK Intellectual Property Office.

The value of intellectual assets as a tool to influence P/E ratio

Over the last 20 or so years, business(es) in general have come to realise that the intellectual assets that a company owns/uses have financial value.

Each particular asset will be of greater value to some than to others. For instance, if your business activity is catering, then a special device to improve the performance of an electrical motor will not be of great significance to you. But to those involved in electrical engineering, such a device could be of monumental importance. Thus, it should be recognised by its owner as a beneficial intellectual asset valuable to those in the electrical engineering industry.

> The trick in attributing some kind of value to your intellectual asset is to match the intellectual asset to a company that would benefit from its ownership.

In Chapter 1 we looked at 'What acquirers look for' from an acquisition. We noted that in many cases acquisition of a company's intellectual assets could be a strategic move for a buyer. It can certainly be a powerful tool in negotiating a high P/E ratio.

The governing factors on this are the actual intellectual assets or intellectual property (IP) themselves.

◆ Does the intellectual asset create 'market control'? In other words, would users have to pay royalties to the owner in order to use the item? Or can it and its peripherals and spares only be obtained from your company, thus giving market control? This makes the asset valuable, with P/E ratio reflecting the extent of the market being controlled and the amount of revenue being raised.

◆ Is the intellectual asset item owned exclusively by your company? If no other companies have this or a similar item, this would put your company in a unique position in the marketplace and would have positive impact on the P/E ratio.

◆ Is the intellectual asset widely publicised and well known? Would an acquirer be buying into a brand ethos? Is the name so well known that acquisition of the company owning this asset would bring kudos and new trade/profit to its owner? To some acquirers this would be influential and attractive, and could result in a high P/E ratio being paid to gain its ownership.

◆ You should undertake marketing activities, and product promotions, to bring recognition and fame to your product and brand.

> Does the intellectual asset have future market potential? How well developed is it? Would ownership and future development bring real business to its owner? Positive answers to this will have positive influence on the P/E ratio.

◆ Are there any potential pitfalls associated with the ownership of your intellectual asset? Is there any other company trading an intellectual asset that you believed to be exclusively yours? This will result in a negative P/E ratio. Acquirers do not want to inherit problems. So address these problem issues early enough to eliminate all negative influences.

Questions acquirers will ask

◆ Is there plenty of opportunity to develop and promote the brand/intellectual asset further?

◆ In purchasing your intellectual assets what special advantage would the acquirer gain?

By evaluating the answers to the questions above you will be able to assess the value of your intellectual assets.

Identifying your company's intellectual assets

Identifying your company's intellectual assets may be easy. For instance, if you are the originator, maker and sole supplier of a 'Special Widget' that is desired by a multitude of clients, then the 'Special Widget' can probably be promoted as an item of intellectual property. Less obvious would be unique computer software that you have written, developed and are supporting. And yet again, maybe a product name which you either could develop or have already developed to become a brand. It could even be your company name that is projected as a brand, thus covering the whole range of products/services that your company supplies (for example, Marks and Spencer/M&S).

Marketing your intellectual property and assets

Marketing intellectual property is all about brand evolution, brand promotion and brand recognition.

> **Brand recognition**
> This is a significant factor in persuading customers to purchase your branded item. Proactive product promotions are important, as is product placement, enabling customers to find and buy the brand easily.

Develop an overall marketing plan

Acquirers/investors will be interested in your marketing plans. For some there may well be particular significance in your methods. Sustainability, market recognition and market penetration can have positive influence on the P/E ratio.

♦ Your intellectual asset marketing strategy should dovetail with your overall exit timing.

♦ It is of significance that you should develop your intellectual assets early in the company evolution, thereby achieving strong trading results during the years leading up to company sale.

♦ Your product range should be making good headway so that you can reduce marketing support during the period before exit.

CHAPTER NINE

Your Company's Business Activity, Logistics and Supply Chain Management

In this chapter:

- *Business activity (or business offering)*
- *Logistics*
- *Procurement and supply chain management*

Business activity (or business offering)

This is the face of the company. It is the part that the public sees, your product range and/or your service activities. It is what your company does in order to earn its living.

> From start up, and through growth of the business, there will have been a lot of experiments. By exit time, experiments should have ceased and the business activity be running efficiently, thus appearing an inviting prospect to buyers. This is particularly pertinent since your business activity is a cost centre. Inefficiencies will waste money. It is this waste that contributes to a reduction in net profitability.

- At exit time the costs of producing and delivering your products or services should have become stabilised, enabling 'selling out' prices of your product range to be reliably calculated.

- 'Production cost control' is essential when creating sales contracts and schemes. Stable costings will be achieved by tight supply chain management.

- Having a clean and tidy workplace presents an image of efficiency to visitors. This will be beneficial to sales when your customers and potential clients visit, selling reliability and high standards.

- At the outset, prospective acquirers/investors will visit your premises. Keeping 'spick and span' all the time, as a matter of routine, means that unexpected visits don't catch you out. And your visitors are impressed by your organisation. A good impression never goes amiss.

> Promote high standards amongst the workforce, and remember to keep your true reasons for 'excellence' a close secret. Any word getting out could jeopardise your plans.

Logistics

Traditionally, logistics covers all aspects of inbound supplies, storage, and outward delivery of goods and services. In other words, materials management.

- Sloppy organisation or poor supervision in this division leads directly to money wasted. This feeds straight to a net profit downturn.

- Too much stock ordered and held until it looks dirty and unsaleable is a story far too often told. Stock poorly stored and hence damaged is another frequent tale, together with goods sent out to clients either too late, or damaged in transit. All of this reflects badly on the company reputation, and translates into net profit reduction.

◆ Inspired management, linked with appropriate computer software that automates ordering, stock holding and outbound delivery, can cure this.

◆ You should resolve to employ well-motivated people with strong characters to manage and supervise this section of the company, and implement system controls that function properly and reliably.

> P/E ratios may be adversely affected by badly managed logistics.

Procurement and supply chain management

From the outset, negotiating keen tariffs and delivery terms with your suppliers is important to the profitability of your venture.

◆ As the company grows, so will the quantity of inventory purchased. This should enable you to claim discounts or rebates from your suppliers.

◆ Negotiating suitable credit terms, and stock delivery arrangements, aids company profit.

◆ Storage buildings cost money. The bigger the building the greater the outlay. Reduce stock holding space and associated costs by getting your suppliers to hold stocks for you, delivering on a 'just in time' basis.

◆ Swift despatch to customers of finished goods means that they can be paid for early, and this improves credit management.

◆ You should investigate outsourcing of some supplies or services since this can produce savings. In outsourcing some activities you can make use of other people's expertise and specialist equipment.

> ### Outsourcing to advantage
> It is not necessary to actually own your fleet of delivery vehicles. Hire them instead. Thus the maintenance and the very many rules regarding vehicular legal compliance are the responsibility of the hire company.

Acquirers will be especially interested in your procurement and supply chain management.

♦ They could gain your advantage if your terms are better than their own procurement terms.

♦ If your terms are not as good as the acquirer's terms of purchasing, they will foresee advantages in bulk buying for your company, when the two companies are merged.

P/E ratios can be influenced by procurement efficiencies.

CHAPTER TEN

Commercial Matters

In this chapter:

- *Importance of commercial matters*
- *Company law and statutory registers*
- *Leases, hire purchase, hire agreements, mortgages and contracts with suppliers*
- *Property leases*
- *Company pensions*
- *Commercial documents*

Importance of commercial matters

Every company, large or small, attracts legal documents, whether it is leases, hire purchase agreements or contracts.

In many companies commercial matters are the province of the company secretary (or head of finance), but it is worth the owner manager becoming *au fait* with commercial matters since this is considered good corporate governance. Some of the commercial information supplied could influence buyers' interest in the company and thereafter affect the P/E ratio.

Company law and statutory registers

It is essential that the company is operating within all laws, including company law.

Compliance falls within the remit of the company secretary.

Records of this compliance must be maintained.

It is important that all Statutory Registers and Returns to Companies House and governmental departments are completed on time and copies retained in up-to-date files. This will even include such documents as insurance, vehicle driving licence copies, and drivers' hours records and tachographs. It goes without saying that tax, wages, NI and pensions must all be dealt with on time.

Leases, hire purchase, hire agreements, mortgages and contracts with suppliers

This covers all property, equipment, plant, machinery, plus vehicles used by the company. All such records must be maintained in an orderly and logical fashion, so that retrieval is an easy matter.

Quite possibly, alterations to, or renegotiation of the duration of, some of your contracts may be necessary to fit in with your exit plans. Beware agreeing to terms of trade that would be too onerous or expensive for new owners to take on. By making early decisions on the exit timetable you will be able to forestall any such problems, making only agreements that are timely with the exit plan.

It is worth you insisting upon seeing every legal document prior to signature by any other member of your staff or your Executive Team. You know this is because you wish to ensure that no document causes problems for exit. You will have to think of an excuse to give to your staff.

Property leases

You should be wary at this point. Many hiccups exist with tenancy leases.

- In principle, if your company is a limited company and the lease is signed in the name of your company then the lease can be transferred to the new owners, assuming its terms allow this.

- To effect this a lawyer will need to prepare a 'licence to assign'.

- However, difficulties will arise if the property lease is signed in your own personal name.

- Where a lease has been signed as a long-term lease – 10, 15, 20 or 25 years – this could give the company the security of location for that period of time. However, the terms do not necessarily automatically allow for new owners to assume the lease.

> The terms of all property leases can be complex and could risk you attracting financial liability or liability regarding assignment, re-assignment and sub-letting. Before any property leases are signed your corporate lawyers should examine them, to see what your precise liabilities are, both at the time of signing and into future years, especially since property and leasing laws seem to change fairly frequently.
> This is the advantage of early appointment of corporate lawyers.

Retail and franchise

See 'Due Diligence, property agreements', page 220.

Both of these operations frequently use property leasing as a means of organising locations from which their business is conducted.

Again, dangers may lurk in the future complexities of these leases, so lawyers should always give advice on each situation as it arises, particularly in the light of your eventual company sale and exit from the business.

Company pensions

Pension funding/under funding has been the downfall of many a proposed deal in recent years. Company pension schemes are continually under review by the government. So compliance with current laws on pensions is essential. Measures should be undertaken to ensure that your pension schemes are not under funded. This will be the first Due Diligence audit, and shortfalls will probably kill any deal with acquirers/investors. Details of all pension schemes fall under the umbrella of 'commercial matters'.

Commercial documents

These will cover every aspect of your business:

◆ property matters;

◆ corporate structure;

◆ suppliers' agreements;

◆ customer agreements;

◆ human resources, director and shareholder agreements;

◆ payroll function;

◆ debt recovery;

◆ governmental returns;

♦ **all the legal documents that the company holds.**

Secure holding of documents

All of the commercial documents should be filed systematically, in subject, date and alphabetical order. Security from fire and theft should be given considerable thought.

Also security within your building, since much of the documentation will be confidential.

CHAPTER ELEVEN

Employee Matters

In this chapter:

- *Think about your employees*
- *Acquirers'/investors' view of employees*
- *Staff pensions*
- *Employment law and human resources specialists*
- *Staff unrest, tribunals, court cases, litigation*
- *Telling staff of the company sale*
- *TUPE – Transfer of Undertakings (Protection of Employment)*
- *Key personnel*
- *IT staff*
- *Staff training*
- *Organisation chart*

Think about your employees

In this day and age you should feel a duty of care for the employees who, without even knowing it, have worked diligently to bring the company to the brink of sale. Thought should be given to the position that staff will find themselves in, following the company sale, since some moral dilemmas exist here for you.

- Your conclusions could well affect your choice of buyer.

- Acquirers/investors will form definite views on each member of your staff.

> Particularly well trained specialist staff are **an asset** of the company. As a team, they could be a valuable asset that buyers are desirous of owning.

Acquirers'/investors' view of employees

There are a number of options for acquirers/investors post acquisition. They could:

- take on all staff and retain them;

- take on all staff for a while, then having reviewed the situation, eliminate some people;

- take on and retain only a few staff (probably key personnel);

- take on selective employees for a settling-down period, in order to maintain client goodwill, and then make them redundant;

- take on none of your staff, which would mean making everyone redundant.

As owner manager your view on this is key to negotiations undertaken by advisers.

- Would you like all staff to be retained? Forever or for how long?

- Do you mind if all staff or just a few are made redundant?

- How will you feel, especially if some employees are your relatives?

- If employees are to be made redundant at the acquisition could this give you some problems?

Give thought to this subject a long time in advance. Inform your corporate finance specialist of your decisions regarding your staff, quite early on. It will affect how he negotiates.

Opportunities exist to safeguard employees.
Build into employees' contracts of employment, **well before sale,** special clauses. For instance, named employees should receive no less than xxx weeks' notice (even up to a year for special people).
But beware. This could put off some acquirers/investors. Especially if the terms are expensive, restrictive or effective over a long period.

Staff pensions

Staff pension funds are a contentious issue in any company sale. The exit strategy planning should address this issue fully and early. A large number of potentially good deals fail because buyers perceive risk attached to the pension fund.

In particular, final salary pension schemes are not popular with acquirers/investors.

You should take pensions advice, years ahead, from corporate financiers and pension advisers. The Government's Pension Regulator should be consulted to avoid post-acquisition claims.

Employment law and human resources (HR) specialists

These days, employment law is complex, ever changing and expensive if the laws are contravened. Most companies of SME size would find it too costly to employ HR specialists on their staff, so find themselves at risk from litigation through ignorance and non compliance.

> Solution – outsource the HR function.

Select a reputable human resources consultancy

◆ You will save yourself much trouble if you select a competent and reputable HR consultancy, who are easy to get on with.

◆ Even so, it is probably best not to discuss your exit plans with anyone in the consultancy.

◆ Select from those with a good reputation, if possible found from networking.

◆ Ask if they guarantee to pay fines, fees, and litigation costs if having followed their advice you find yourself in court.

◆ Check out the list of what they do for you.

◆ Compare with a second company to see that all matters are covered.

> Discipline and grievance matters are disruptive, and hugely expensive.

◆ The HR consultant should be on hand 24/7 to guide you through issues that may 'blow up'.

◆ Should an incident flare up, they should talk you through a preventative course of action.

◆ Provided you follow their advice to the letter, any litigation that results in court/tribunal action with fines imposed should be handled by them. Generally, they fund both legal costs and fines in such circumstances.

- Contracts of employment for all staff can be drawn up by the HR consultancy, and updated as laws change.

> Outsourcing this vital function leaves you free to continue building the company, and demonstrates that your company is making efforts to comply with employment law.

- HR specialists undertake to guide you through the maze of legislation, by preparing compliant staff contracts of employment for each member of staff. They also keep you abreast of all legislation to include: working time; holidays; health and safety; discrimination and diversity; drivers' regulations; HR strategy; industrial and employee relations; maternity and paternity issues; pay and benefits; termination of employment; training and development; plus any other pertinent matters.

- Their fees are charged in relation to employee numbers.

- Using HR consultants' services gives an element of protection from litigation because you have in effect 'passed the problems on'.

> Acquirers/investors are used to outsourced HR contracts, which they view as sensible. They too can benefit from the umbrella of protection given by the outsourcing company's earlier involvement.

> **Remember**
> Litigation, and tribunals, can be brought against businesses, not only by employees, but also by **job applicants**. Include this aspect in your HR consultancy contract.

Staff unrest, tribunals, court cases, litigation

This is a really big turn off for any buyer.

It is much better to resolve legal disputes and claims, 'in full and final settlement', in advance of sale time almost regardless of the rights or wrongs of the case. By doing this the dispute is removed from the buyer's concern.

Additionally, staff unrest, disagreements and lack of harmony must be addressed well ahead of sale time. No buyer wants the risk factor of trouble pending. In the visits to your premises, during Due Diligence, your people will be covertly appraised. Any air of disunity, friction, or bad feeling will be reported back to buyers. This could adversely affect the deal. So try to run a 'happy ship'.

Telling staff of the company sale

This is a sensitive subject, upon which everyone will have a view. Fear for their future is the most dominant emotion, together with worries regarding wages, perks and status.

Telling staff before completion risks the deal failing.

However, if your deal is subject to TUPE regulations coming into force there are guidelines that must be followed. (See TUPE below.)

Part of the negotiations with buyers will centre on when to tell staff. It is common practice for a mutually agreed statement to be produced. The announcement to staff following completion is delivered at a prearranged time and place by agreed individuals. This is the 'hand-over' ceremony, in which you will undoubtedly play an important part.

> **Acquainting employees with all of the information is a critical subject that should be handled sensitively.**

Badly informed employees risk losing clients, resulting in escrow payments to shareholders being withheld.

TUPE – Transfer of Undertakings (Protection of Employment)

There are some deals where TUPE is enforced and others where the type of deal agreed means that it is not enforced. Advisers must keep you abreast of the situation and advise of any action necessary on your part, because TUPE regulations insist that employees and their representatives have the right to know and the right to be consulted '**once a deal is certain to complete**'. However, there are many occasions when, even at the last, the deal may not actually complete.

> **You must take advice from your lawyers on this very tricky subject.**

However, don't tell employees unless you are certain that you are obliged to do so in law.

Key personnel

Key personnel are people who hold strategic posts within the company. They are probably part of your Executive Team, but are not necessarily policy decision makers. For instance, your information technology (IT) manager He will be crucially involved in keeping the IT system running and secure, but not necessarily involved in policy decisions for the company.

Because their positions are key to achievement of 'targets on time' and the satisfactory running of your business, it is clearly necessary to keep them happy and well motivated. Should they decide to leave, especially if lured away by competitors, confidential and key information may be in jeopardy.

Losing key employees does not send out good messages about the company. It is worthwhile devising ways of 'locking' them in to your company.

> There is a fine judgement for you as owner manager here.
> You need to reward key staff well, so that they are motivated and happy, but not so high that the axe falls on them quickly after sale.
> At all costs, even though they are key individuals, do not reveal to them your intention to sell the company prior to sale completion.

IT staff

The subject of IT staff, especially the head of IT, can give owner managers sleepless nights.

* Companies can be at the mercy of disaffected IT staff. Any resultant alteration or deletion of data, or programs mischievously adapted, can cause critical harm.

* IT staff discovering a pending company sale could cause tremendous damage if they chose. The only answer is to keep them all well motivated, happy and well paid.

◆ You could keep a computer back up in your possession as a safety measure, but this will always be out of date, as daily transactions are completed.

◆ The head of IT will be required to produce reams of customised reports and information at the Due Diligence stage of negotiations, and if a merger of computing systems is on the cards, he will be involved in discussion with the new company's IT staff.

Head of IT
When offers are made to buy the company and the negotiations are actually in progress the head of IT should be informed. To keep him 'onside', and to preserve secrecy, some incentive should be offered.
For instance, £xxx bonus at sale completion.
A really good working relationship between owner manager and IT head is often critical to company development as well as a successful sale completion.
It is generally a good idea to allow the head of IT to report directly to the owner manager in the same fashion as company directors.

Staff training

Your employees are your jewels, and can in their own right be an asset that other companies may covet. It is therefore worth training all individuals to do their job to the very best of their ability.

The company will benefit from better performance that can feed right through to extra turnover. We have all been to a shop where we've been told 'if it isn't on the shelf we haven't got it'. We feel let down. So, when we find a place that looks after our requirements, makes us feel special and, above all, satisfies our needs as customers, we tend to return.

Training can be done 'in house' or at outsourced training companies. The latter will always be expensive. So why not employ and train **your own trainer**, applying for training grants and development schemes to help to cover the costs involved. This is the winner all round. To acquirers/investors this indicates a well run organisation, which will have a positive influence on the P/E ratio.

Organisation chart

An organisation chart is always a good thing to have, depicting reporting lines, and demonstrating to everyone exactly how their job fits into the company as a whole. This chart is an echo of your management structure chart (see page 88), showing each individual's job, and their reporting lines. From managing director to cleaner it is easy to see how the company is constructed.

It can be a motivational tool, allowing staff to see at a glance how their career paths can progress. Each person's job should be given a title, job description and information on their status within the company. A management structure chart does this very well.

CHAPTER TWELVE

Information Technology

In this chapter:

- *The importance of information technology*
- *Choosing hardware and software*
- *'In house' or outsourced system support?*
- *IT security*
- *Licensing*
- *IT systems as a company asset*
- *Integration with acquirer's system*
- *Head of IT*

The importance of information technology

These days there can be very few companies that are being run without a computer. At start up this will comprise a simple computer hardware and software system, recording customer data, and possibly simple accountancy. In many companies it will be referred to as your 'information system'.

But as your company grows you would be wise to investigate the most appropriate hardware and software systems that will carry you forward into the future. They must take you efficiently through your growth, enabling the collection, storage, interrogation and manipulation of your company's information, which will be key to the long road towards expansion then exit.

Choosing hardware and software

Being a wise computer customer you will no doubt choose both the most appropriate software and the hardware to run it from one single supplier. This avoids suppliers playing the 'blame game', such as 'The hardware is OK, it's the software at fault', or vice versa. If there is only **one** supplier it is down to him to choose compatible systems, and to correct whatever faults arise.

Take time, a long time, to select your software. Decide what you really want it to do, not what computer companies tell you you should have. Don't let computer companies talk jargon and 'computerese' at you. This is merely a means of confusing you, and you will miss out on vital points. Insist on plain English explanations. You should see what is available 'off the peg' so to speak.

Select software that is adaptable to meet your needs, and can be customised by software suppliers to suit your requirements. Decide what you really want from your computer. Devise methods, procedures and techniques that work manually first. If it can't work manually, it probably won't work on a computer.

Visit other companies that you think are successfully using their system to do what you want to do. Make it clear you are not trying to copy their product lines, etc., or 'steal' their customers and you will generally be welcomed by companies proud to show their success.

Check out trade magazines, exhibitions, computer software and hardware houses, networking and newspaper stories to see what other companies, quite often in different lines of work, are achieving. Be diligent about this, take your time. You will often learn about things that you don't want to do. This is useful in selecting your software. Choose up-to-date, not 'becoming outdated', systems.

> A software system that will allow you to interrogate data and customise reports etc., is a must. Marketing, management accounts and Due Diligence depend on this.

A system that is totally integrated throughout all departments of the company is extremely desirable, and will delight auditing accountants. You will have peace of mind that staff can't easily cheat the system. Integrated systems will save auditing fees because there is less work for accountants to do. It is wise to select a system that is well known to accountants by its brand name.

You are about to spend huge amounts of money on your information technology. Your bank may help. They will certainly understand. But you may find the expenditure is so high that it requires grants, business angels or even equity support. You will need to describe to proposed lenders, accurately, what the system does, and how your business will benefit.

Your auditing accountants will present the expenditure and purchase of your IT system in your accounts in such a fashion that it is an asset. But check out depreciation times.

Is your trading year 12 months or 13 x 4 week periods?
Decisions on this factor should be made well before choosing your IT software. Management accounts should direct this. Remember,

this accountancy factor is crucial, because some systems cannot operate a 13-period year.

'In house' or outsourced system support?

In general, your technical support is best provided by the suppliers of your hardware and software.

However, a competent head of IT with training from these suppliers will be able to supplement their work with small 'fixes', which has the benefit of immediacy. Fixing the problems as they arise will keep your system running and reduce downtime.

IT security

IT security is a subject that can terrify owner managers. It is certainly a matter for the board of directors, since breached security causes danger, not only to your IT system itself, but possibly to the company as a whole.

As computers become ever more sophisticated their uses increase, but so do the security dangers coming from: infiltration by hackers; disaffected staff; offsite access to your system; accidental or malicious damage; system breakdown.

It is sensible that you develop risk management policies to counteract these problems. Keeping up to date with potential IT threats is a must. This will be analysed at Due Diligence, to ascertain whether your information remains secure within your firm, or has entered the public domain where its release would undermine an acquirer's plans.

Licensing

To 'non-techy' people it will come as a shock just how many IT licences are needed to run your system. Today there are firms whose job it is to check that all licences are obtained. There are penalties for non-compliance, which could disrupt your smooth running if you have been deliberately non-compliant. Check out your licences. If they are out of date or non-existent you risk litigation.

Your IT systems as a company asset

Your auditing accountant will want to record both your hardware and software when newly installed as assets, particularly if you have borrowed to fund this installation. If you possess some specially developed software, unusual or particularly pertinent and unique to your business, it could be thought of as an asset when company sale prices are negotiated. Thus it is possible that some software systems could affect the P/E ratio.

Integration with your acquirer's IT system

Acquirers who plan to purchase your company in order to merge it with others in their ownership may wish to integrate your system into theirs or vice versa. This could prove a topic for discussion at the negotiations. Discussion with your corporate finance specialist will discern whether there is any mileage in this. Your head of IT should also be consulted.

Head of IT

This is a person who is really important in keeping your IT systems running properly, and securely, and who will be an essential member of your team at company exit time.

Because you will require them to be expert in your systems you should ensure that they are fully trained by both the hardware and software houses. This training should be continually updated.

If you can develop a good rapport with the head of IT this is a sensible working precaution against problems. Allowing him to report directly to you should nurture understanding.

As your company grows you will need the computer to conduct transactions, record specific information and control various activities. Involvement of the IT manager in all growth aspects is imperative.

CHAPTER THIRTEEN

Reputation

In this chapter:

- *Personal reputation*
- *Company reputation*
- *Mission statement*
- *The effect of reputation on your P/E ratio*

Personal reputation

This is the one factor that you as owner manager are likely to overlook, or be one upon which you will be unable to pass realistic judgement. But acquirers/investors will certainly be checking you out. If you seem 'slick', or untrustworthy, there may be reluctance to begin negotiations. Remember, buyers don't like risk.

Company reputation

Your customers will increase if the company reputation is good. We are all aware of the 'Del Boy' image, and find ourselves reluctant to trade with such businesses, in case we are ripped off. We would rather spend with reputable dealers, where we know that if the goods 'go wrong', we can return them and be treated fairly. Your business will grow more quickly if you are an honest, straightforward trader.

In building a brand image, it is a good reputation that is the most influential fact. This is one reason why we choose the more expensive, well advertised branded product, rather than an unknown product that we feel uncertain about.

Your company reputation and good name are valuable. In the words of the old saying, 'It takes a long time to build a good name, but only a moment to destroy'.

Mission statement

The modern cult of 'mission statements' is a way of describing to the world that your company trades with customers, suppliers and staff fairly and honestly. In these days of awareness of human rights it makes sense to pronounce to the world, via your mission statement, that you treat everyone decently and honourably.

Your mission statement should declare where your company stands on moral and ethical issues. Of growing importance are the 'green' issues. Thus it is sensible to declare your standing on climate change, carbon footprint and ecologically important issues.

The effect of reputation on your P/E ratio

Your reputation will prove to be important to investors, who will want the company to continue trading as now. The future potential of the company and its current image will be important to those willing to invest.

It is both your own and the company's reputation that will be influential in the matters of warranties, guarantees and indemnities. If buyers feel insecure it is probable that the warranties will cover a large sum withheld in escrow accounts, and the length of time of this withholding may be long.

CHAPTER FOURTEEN

Your Pre-sale Period

In this chapter:

- *When is pre-sale?*
- *Share buy back*
- *Eliminating all non-essential expenditure*
- *Straightening out the books*
- *Making the market aware*

When is pre-sale?

Your **pre-sale** time is the period prior to your planned **exit** that allows you to position everything to advantage and present the company well.

> ### The pre-sale period
> If you were selling your house it's the time just prior to calling in the estate agents, when you are painting the rooms and tidying the garden ready to attract lots of buyers and get the best price.

There are a number of activities to undertake or 'see to', all of them designed to maximise your profit, thus impressing and attracting buyers. This pre-sale period is not a date, or set in stone. You will identify the time to begin your pre-sale activities by looking at your management accounts, the company's efficiencies, and position in your chosen marketplaces. You will know when the time is right.

Of course, consultation with your exit timetable will be influential in making this decision.

See 'Exit time plan', page 60.

> The pre-sale window is the time to maximise net profit…both £££ and percentage.

No doubt you will have already begun preparations by getting your annual accounts independently audited over the last few years. Now look at your finances, in relation to your financial supporters. How satisfactory is the situation? Is your cash at bank building up?

Private equity and business angels' loans during the pre-exit phase

In the formative and growth years you may well have been grateful for the substantial support received from a venture capital or business angel. Private equity and business angels are superb at taking on the risk factors of an emerging business.

However, as time goes by and the business becomes successful, the enhanced repayment terms of the equity loan can become a burden, and substantially reduce your profit, slowing the pace of your financial growth.

During your pre-sale window, the equity loan will considerably and excessively reduce the profit of the company, just when you are trying to show large profit figures and increase that cash at bank.

> One solution is to 'buy back' your shares (called unsurprisingly a 'shares buy back'). This comprises replacing the equity loan with a **non-equity loan.**

Shares buy back

Contracts with private equity and business angels loans are

frequently constrained by terms that introduce 'compensatory dividends' and the like. These compel your company to give funds additional to the regular repayment schedule, and dividend payments, to the lenders, in the event of your directors and shareholders receiving enhanced remuneration in cash or kind.

You can change the situation by **buying back** the company's shares from the investor concerned, and take on, instead, a more straightforward and less expensive repayment loan from a bank or similar.

> Replacing private equity loans is usually accompanied by a clause entitled 'no embarrassment'. This means that within a specified period of time (usually one year) the company must not be sold to another private buyer or investment company. Should such a sale 'complete' within the 'no embarrassment' period, financial penalties will ensue. So calculate when you should begin to negotiate your shares buy back.

Financial assistance may be needed to complete this audacious move. The recent changes to the Companies Act have affected the procedures that must be followed. So, to complete a shares buy back, it is essential that you consult with both your corporate lawyers, and corporate finance specialists beforehand. This is probably the first move to make in your pre-sale window, if you are to do it at all.

> Negotiating exit sale terms will be much easier without interference from private equity shareholders. Indeed, as a shareholder of your company, a private equity partner would be entitled to a percentage of the sale proceeds, equal to their percentage shareholding and as per your Articles of Association. This would deplete your own sales receipts very considerably.

Eliminating all non-essential expenditure

This is your next activity in the pre-sale period, thus making savings that feed directly through to bottom line profit.

◆ You could perhaps make savings on exhibitions, or non-essential advertising.

◆ If the company is carrying a surplus of staff, consider merging some positions to save on staff wages.

◆ Look also at superfluous equipment, vehicles, stock, buildings, and find ways to eliminate/reduce these costs.

◆ Find ways to reduce outgoings without reducing sales.

> **Important**
> Take pre-sale advice from your auditing accountant to present the audited accounts in the most attractive light by moving items in the balance sheet and profit and loss account to show increased value.

Straightening out the books

◆ Straighten out any tax avoidance schemes. These will be viewed with mistrust by buyers.

◆ Indeed, if a company is to look profitable (and that is what attracts buyers), then taxes will be due. Bite the bullet and declare at least three years' profit before proposed exit.

◆ Complex company structures such as holding companies, subsidiaries, franchises and so on may need attention. **Take advice from auditing accountants and corporate financiers.**

- Pension schemes **must** hold sufficient funds. Apply for clearance from the Government Pension Regulator in order to eliminate claims post-sale.

- You should query your property leases with your lawyers. You are looking for the complications of leases with continuing liability, or guarantor liability. Both of these leases are somewhat complicated for this book, but do have power to harm your exit if not dealt with early and properly.

- Disentangle director borrowings and perks, especially houses, boats, land, property, etc. These matters will be noted at Due Diligence stage, and can be taken care of during negotiations, but they will generally have the effect of reducing the P/E ratio.

- Sort out stock inventory. Don't hold too much stock: it is better held as cash at bank. Old, slow-moving or obsolete stock is often better written off by you, rather than by purchasers who will simply compensate by reducing the price paid for the company.

- Sort out debtor problems. Write off bad debts yourself, prior to sale, or the price paid for the company will suffer. You can still press for payment even after write off. You could be lucky.

- Ensure all accountancy records and movements are legal, and within company law.

- Springclean buildings, vehicles, equipment, and land, to give good appearance and increased valuation.

- Ensure all matters of actual or threatened litigation are cleared up in the pre-exit phase. This will cover everything from disagreements with suppliers over payment, delivery or quality of goods that could later turn nasty. It could be relations with staff, or interviewees, where unrest is likely to become a litigation or tribunal matter. It could be disagreements with customers over the products, the manner in which they were delivered, the quality or type of service that a customer feels was not carried out as expected. It could even be vehicle and transport regulations flouted, or accidents caused or being claimed for by someone. In running a business there are opportunities for disagreement all around that if left unattended will become 'issues' or matters for litigation. Examine every aspect of your business in close detail during this window pre-sale.

> Buyers do not like litigation, either actual or threatened. It could prove a deal breaker. So, back down and settle matters with the complainant if you wish to go forward to sale.

◆ Due Diligence examination will expose and interrogate company matters in the finest of detail. The pre-sale period is the time to prepare for this.

◆ Straighten out all tax and customs affairs with HMRC. Getting tax clearance is a good move.

◆ Similarly, straighten out all National Insurance and payroll issues.

> Spin off any businesses or operations that are not part of the main core business. This could be unsettling to buyers. So eliminate these distractions whilst there is time to do so.

Making the market aware

The company is now prepared, the books look attractive, the business is progressing and on target to reach its projections, so you are nearly ready. You still must not discuss your proposals to exit with staff, but you can now talk to your corporate advisers, telling them you are about ready to move.

You can prepare a private Information Memorandum, ready to issue to your corporate financier when someone expresses interest. This document tells prospective buyers the facts and features of your business, so that they can decide whether this is of interest to them.

Networking should be undertaken by you, telling people that your business is doing well. Do not actually ask if prospects are interested in buying you out. To do so would lose negotiating advantage. But hints along the lines of 'I'm nearly ready for retirement' or 'I'd like to go abroad to live' may fall on the right ears. It is quite surprising how gossip circulates, and as long as you are vague, but stressing your company success, someone is bound to surface. Trade shows and industry body events are the best places to meet someone who could be interested as a trade buyer. If networking does not produce interested parties, your corporate finance specialist is well situated to seek out buyers for you.

> Do not put adverts in the newspapers yourself. Leave this to the professionals.

CHAPTER FIFTEEN

The Company Sale Process

In this chapter:

- *Enter the professionals*
- *Personal taxation*
- *Confidentiality agreements*
- *Offers to buy the company*
- *Heads of Terms*
- *The structure of the deal*
- *Sale and purchase agreement*
- *'Lock ins'*

Enter the professionals

You have entered a key stage in your exit, the time when you must let your experienced advisers take over.

- This indicates to purchasers that matters will be dealt with lawfully, expediently and efficiently by experts. You are not a push-over, ready to give away your company for a pittance.

- Time wasters will be 'sussed out' and tactfully eliminated by your professional advisers, before confidential information is needlessly released.

- Your professionals will draw up all of the preliminary documents necessary to proceed to negotiations.

- They will decide on, construct and negotiate the deal that is best for you.

- Your corporate lawyers begin work with your corporate finance specialists to produce the sale documentation involved, including the sale and purchase agreement.

- They all become heavily involved with the representatives of 'the other side', in Due Diligence questions, answers and disclosures.

- It is possible that several suitors may hold preliminary discussions with your advisers, wherein offers that do not meet your objectives are put forward. It is sensible to decline unsuitable propositions gracefully. Don't close any doors. You never know what the future may hold. Re-negotiations are always possible with the passage of time, and can be originated from either side.

Sales negotiations appear to go on forever.
It seems that as soon as an acceptable deal is found,
a problem arises to kill that version.
There are many false stops and restarts.
This is normal.
So hold your nerve and let the professionals keep negotiating.

Keep the company running to target. Allow your Executive Team to take this strain.
This is the most important aspect of this time.
Lots of deals fail to complete, because the owner manager has taken his eye off the ball leading to a dip in sales.
The impact is a reduced sale price, or changed terms, often a loss of sales proceeds.

Liaising with your advisers

It essential that all advisers know in detail at the outset what you expect from the sale.

Personal taxation

As mentioned many times before, tax planning will figure heavily and in many situations actually drive the format and timing of the deal. After all, it is how much you can keep (not give to the tax man), that will form the platform of your wealth.

It is thus critical that you should consult tax specialists **even during the course of the sale negotiations**. Your age, your aspirations, current company structure, your aims, particularly if yours is a family company, will all have bearing on the most suitable personal tax plan. This plan will translate into the best type of deal for you, whether for instance it should be an 'all shares deal' or perhaps another construction.

Tax specialists are able to review your current and past tax history and, looking at what is allowed for forthcoming years, give sound advice. This advice should be communicated to your corporate finance specialist. The tax position can often be so complicated to those who are not specialist in tax matters that it is a good idea for these two experts to converse together, prior to the deal construction.

It is probable that the tax position of other shareholders may also be discussed, so that no one is disadvantaged by the sale.

Confidentiality agreement

This may elsewhere be described as a non-disclosure agreement.

- Every business owner is paranoid about retaining company 'secrets'.

- As we saw in Chapter 1, confidentiality could be the key to the successful outcome of a proposed sale.

- So, at the outset, probably before circulating in-depth company information, your corporate advisers will ask prospective purchasers to sign a 'confidentiality agreement'.

- This document is designed to prevent prospective acquirers/ investors from divulging that your company (by name) is for sale, and to prevent revelations of the confidential information provided to him.

- It is notoriously difficult to enforce a confidentiality agreement in any court case of 'breach of confidence'. However, it does discourage a suitor from casual disclosure. Its introduction indicates that you are about to take his offer seriously, and expect him to treat as confidential all information provided.

> Do not put too much faith in these confidentiality agreements;
> they are not to be completely trusted.
> Loose talk can be encountered on both sides.

Offers to buy the company

Wherever interest is raised in your company all approaches and offers should be put in writing to your corporate finance specialist.
Do not be tempted to engage in conversation yourself, and definitely never discuss or suggest a price.
Do suggest that any casual offers are put in writing to you
(for you to forward to advisers).
This sorts out the genuinely interested buyer from the 'not really interested'.

Using preliminary written offers your adviser can begin negotiations. An early move he will make is to produce 'Heads of Terms' (or 'Heads of Agreement').

Heads of Terms

Heads of Terms is a document that could best be described as a 'letter of intent'. It should only be raised by corporate advisers, because of the complications and implications within its content. **Don't do this yourself.**

In principle, it is a document setting out the preliminary terms of negotiation, plus a very broad structure of the proposed deal. It could well contain terms to protect the confidentiality of the information that will be disclosed in the course of negotiations and Due Diligence.

There may be conditions proposed regarding costs if the deal does not progress to completion. There may/or may not be terms regarding a 'lock out'. That is a set period of time during which exclusivity is granted to one prospective buyer whilst he scrutinises your company, and restricts availability of information to other buyers during this period. Some deals may not have this 'lock out' clause. It all depends on the negotiations in hand.

> Basically, Heads of Terms is a preliminary document, a 'road map' to the procedures of the hard negotiating to follow.
> A comprehensive Heads of Terms document, drawn up by the corporate advisers, will give buyers less room to manoeuvre later on, or to try to adjust a deal, or change its terms. Your corporate advisers will draw up the most appropriate for your circumstances.

> After the Heads of Terms have been signed Due Diligence begins.
> It is common for a period of some 45–90 days to be allowed for the deal to complete. Thereafter, it is always possible to extend the period as necessary.

The structure of the deal

By now you will be much clearer about your preferred objectives, by knowing who is making offers.

- Do you wish to sell the company complete?

- Do you wish to sell the trading business, whilst retaining ownership of land, property, or intellectual assets such as brand names?

- Do you wish to pass on to, or sell any part of the business to family members, now or in the future?

Also:

- In taking tax specialist advice have you given due consideration to all aspects of capital gains tax, inheritance tax, tax relief and pension?

◆ Your pre-sale planning should have taken account of matters such as grants, leases, contracts, agreements, licences and franchise agreements. In your preparations it is necessary to see if these contracts, leases, agreements, etc., can be assigned, or if other legal arrangements or changes are necessary to go forward to sale.

Share purchase

Share purchase is a deal in which the acquirers/investors purchase the shares of the company thus the business and all connected with it are sold complete. This is the most straightforward deal for the vendor, being completed in one contract of sale.

However, this deal type may not be the one buyers prefer. It may not for them be the most tax efficient, or there may be hidden undisclosed liabilities that surface after acquisition and after escrow release. This is for your corporate advisers to negotiate on your behalf. It is one of the many reasons why you need 'top notch' professionals.

◆ This deal is subject to capital gains tax, for the recipients of the sale proceeds (the shareholders).

◆ Because the purchaser is assuming the liabilities of the company, Due Diligence is likely to be very stringent.

◆ Warranties and indemnities are instituted to cover perceived risk, and may be in force for a considerable time after completion.

Trade and asset purchase

Trade and asset purchase describes selling the trading business and its assets, both tangible and intangible, but does not sell 'the company'. For a vendor seeking to retire from business totally, a later transaction is necessary, in which 'the company' is liquidated, transferred or sold separately.

In this 'asset deal' each asset will require separate legal transfer, together with possible renewal and renegotiation of any associated legal agreements.

To vendors, the hazard of capital gains tax is payable by 'the company' at the sale of the assets. This means there is a reduced amount available to shareholders of the company. And when they finally receive their sale proceeds from the disposal of 'the company', another capital gains tax bill is due. In other words, shareholders are taxed twice.

Covenants

As the final stages of negotiations are reached, discussions on the price and terms of the sale will conclude with the subject of 'the sellers' employment following the sale'. Buyers do not want sellers walking away with sale proceeds, only to set up in competition soon after the sale. Nor do they want a seller to take confidential information and use it in competition against the buyer.

So, restrictions are put on these individuals by way of covenants, mutually agreed and accepted in the course of negotiations. These covenants can cover a number of situations appropriate to each individual set of circumstances. Lawyers will supervise the wording of these clauses. Typically, a seller will covenant not to work in competing industry for a period of xxx years.

Sale and purchase agreement

This is the document that transfers ownership from the seller to the buyer and progresses everyone towards finality of proceedings.

Summarised within the document will be the price, the terms and conditions of the sale, the participants' names, warranties, indemnities, guarantees, disclosures in the form of a disclosure letter, ongoing confidentiality covenants, details and terms of escrow accounts, plus all other conditions and covenants that have been negotiated. This document is the culmination of weeks of work and discussion.

The sale process will be completed by the signatures of all concerned, on the document, together with the movement of funds from the buyer's to the seller's accountants for onward distribution.

Warranties, guarantees, indemnities

You will be required to formally sign a document declaring that the information provided to the acquirer/investor is correct and complete, and that you can see no reason for any 'loss of trade' post-sale, or any other damaging circumstance arising.

- Warranties are the statements made about the company and its state of affairs.

- Guarantees are statements declaring that there are no unfortunate or unstated situations that will arise in the future.

See 'Escrow accounts', Chapter 17, page 239.

- Indemnities require you to make good to the acquirer/investor any loss that he should suffer if you have sold the company to him, knowing of circumstances that could lead to the purchaser incurring financial loss.

◆ Due Diligence leads on to the measurement of warranties, guarantees and indemnities by the buyer that could in a few deals be translated into the escrow account.

'Lock ins'

You will know that there will be some deals that are contingent upon you personally remaining within the company:

◆ to ensure a smooth transfer of ownership;

◆ to reassure customers that they will be serviced as per their usual arrangement;

◆ to give new staff a chance to settle in and understand the nuances of the company;

◆ to reassure existing staff, so that they do not leave.

The advantages of your 'lock in' are all with the buyer.

> **If you are subject to a 'lock in'**
> As far as you are concerned: you are no longer your own boss; you will have to account for your time; you can no longer sanction major expenditure; you can no longer set the politics – that is down to the new owners; you can no longer set the targets – these are set by the new owners; you will have to adapt to great change.

So, when negotiating your terms of 'lock in' make them as short as possible.

At negotiation, try to get a firm closure date put on this period. Ensure you negotiate written terms of engagement as follows.

- What is your job title?

- Make sure there is a service agreement.

- Who do you report to?

- What are your responsibilities?

- What are the limitations on your authority?

- What is your remuneration, whether this is to include commissions, expenses, car, pension etc?

- Will you be rewarded for outperforming targets set?

- Is your final release contingent on targets being met? If so, what level of authority do you have in order to meet these targets?

- What role will you play in merging the operation of the two companies after the sale?

There will be many other points that you will wish to cover before agreeing to the role on offer.

By now the sale process discussions should be nearing their end.

The sale has been negotiated and is now awaiting completion.

CHAPTER SIXTEEN

Introducing Due Diligence

In this chapter:

- *What is the Due Diligence investigation?*
- *The impact of the Due Diligence investigation*
- *Should you hold back information?*
- *You will find Due Diligence difficult*
- *Keep track of your replies*
- *Disclosures*
- *When does Due Diligence take place?*
- *The scope of Due Diligence*
- *Prepare in advance*

What is the Due Diligence investigation?

For you, just as for all other owner managers, Due Diligence is the oft-heralded 'nightmare'. It is a rigorous and extremely probing examination asking questions about every aspect of the affairs of your company. It occurs at the time of a refinancing operation, or company sale. The information requested covers past years, the present time, and commitments into the future made by the company and its representatives.

Due Diligence requires you to provide 'full and fair disclosure' in response to all questions. You will find this investigation is disrupting, disturbing and possibly frustrating. But it is an essential step that buyers or investors will always take.

> You should know about Due Diligence very early on in your company evolution. Sometime, somehow, it is a process that will surface. Clever and careful organisation of your company records from the early days can make the process less arduous.

The impact of the Due Diligence investigation

Due Diligence is the part of your negotiations which allows a prospective acquirer/investor to gain reassurance that your company is a viable proposition **with minimal risk attached**. The results of the Due Diligence analysis will have dramatic repercussions:

- The acquirer/investor confirms his interest.

- The acquirer/investor becomes nervous about the company.

- The acquirer/investor may be persuaded to pay more for the company.

- The acquirer/investor reduces his bid price.

- The acquirer/investor constructs the deal differently.

- The acquirer/investor withdraws all offers.

- Acquirers/investors evaluate various degrees of post-sale indemnities, warranties and guarantees that will translate into escrow accounts.

Caution

You will be naturally nervous that revealing sensitive information can have the following results:

◆ Exposure of confidential company matters to outsiders could damage future trading if the deal should not proceed to completion.

◆ Unscrupulous acquirers could feign interest in your company and its methods, find out all they can via Due Diligence examination then, having withdrawn from negotiations, go off to set up a similar competing operation.

Be wary

Being such an interrogative process, you should treat Due Diligence with caution, releasing only fairly general information. It would be sensible at this stage to hold a discussion with your corporate advisers about the precise disclosure of the 'sensitive data' that will be requested. Build a strategy for disclosures with your corporate advisers, then follow it very closely. When in doubt, check with them. Each company will be different as to what could be damaging to its future operations, in the event of the deal not completing.

But be fair
Equally, it is only reasonable that buyers know what they are letting themselves in for. So, bite the bullet and tread a fine line of declarations and disclosures during Due Diligence.

Should you hold back information?

There will be a natural reluctance to tell buyers some information in case the deal is killed off by its revelation. It would be tempting to keep quiet if you are aware that a client's contract is not going to be renewed. Or perhaps that some of the stock in your warehouse is damaged and of no real value. Holding back such information would be pointless, because you will later be asked directly if you know of any such situations.

You will be required to give indemnities and warranties against misleading or inaccurate replies. Don't be tempted to give partial or incorrect replies. It is much better to give full disclosure, but keeping these replies low key, without any undue emphasis that would be discouraging to buyers.

Be open and honest with your advisers from a very early stage, pointing out aspects that you believe could be problematical to the deal so that they are prepared for these difficulties. Corporate advisers hate 'nasty surprises'.

Due Diligence is a pain that will have to be endured if the deal is to proceed.

> An unsatisfactory Due Diligence outcome may mean 'the deal is off'.

You will find Due Diligence difficult

The Due Diligence investigation is undertaken by the 'other side', employing advisers who are professional accountants and lawyers. If your enterprise is a speciality, the auditors will use experts in that special field. These representatives of the acquirer/investor aim to investigate the company in such a fashion that risk factors are flushed out. They act to determine that all statements made by, or on behalf of your company, are true, accurate and complete.

Due Diligence (as it is commonly termed) is physically disturbing for you because immense amounts of information will be requested, which need reply within very short time frames. Much research into long forgotten facts may prove time consuming and could become disrupting to the company's everyday business while the effort is made to discover the answers (or even discover where the answers are stored).

Due Diligence is mentally disturbing because it is all conducted 'secretly'. Your staff in general can't be involved, and thus it all seems furtive. So deep and probing are some of the questions (as is the whole process) that there is a tendency to feel guilty, even though you have nothing to feel guilty about – much like feeling guilty when you see a policeman.

Huge amounts of data will need to be gathered, prepared and replied to out of hours. The whole process seems to go on forever. And just when you think it's all over another lot of questions arrive.

Ensure you have your Executive Team in place, to run the everyday affairs of the company and meet the previously stated targets, leaving you free to deal with Due Diligence.

It is crucial to keep the company running and on target.

> The bigger the deal, the more stringent the investigation.

Keep track of your replies

It is a sensible precaution to reply to Due Diligence questions in writing as far as possible. This is referred to as 'providing disclosure'. From the outset keep copies of disclosures, filing in logical order for easy retrieval. Keep any other Due Diligence correspondence similarly filed and away from employees' casual glance.

You may find that apparently the same question will be asked more than once, first by the accountants, then by the lawyers. Each will be seeking a different standpoint from your reply. But it is obvious that you should give the same reply to the question.

Hard copy replies can easily be referred to at later points during negotiation, and are better than verbal replies that can be misunderstood or misconstrued. However, if you do have to make verbal responses these should be 'written up' and filed along with your other documents. It is a good idea to let your advisers see your responses before returning them to the auditors, although response times may be very short.

> Should the sale not proceed to completion, all the information supplied to the other side should be returned to you. Your advisers will probably have written a clause into the Confidentiality Agreement that requires the other side to 'deliver up' or destroy all Due Diligence replies.
> However, the genie is now out of the bottle.
> Confidentiality can't be relied upon.

> Because the whole process of Due Diligence and company sale is still secret, a code name may be agreed upon by advisers, for instance 'Project Palace' (to be used in requesting and supplying information). Visits by your buyers' representatives and the very many other 'suits' involved will need to be discreet. If you can develop a cover story for all of this you may be lucky in keeping up the secret.
> A good subterfuge is talking to advisers about getting extra investment for faster growth.

Disclosures

The answers to the thousands of questions that you will be asked during Due Diligence will be considered as 'disclosures', in that 'you are disclosing xxxx information' to the acquirers/investors.

♦ Additionally, a letter in which you make statements to clarify your replies is called your 'disclosures letter'.

♦ The purpose of disclosures: acquirers/investors will evaluate the disclosed information when coming to a decision on whether or not to purchase, and on the price/structure of the deal.

> Disclosures made in writing to acquirers/investors 'presale' cannot form the basis of an objection or claim by those same purchasers for rebate or compensation, 'post sale'.
> The other side will prepare edited copies for you in the form of a 'bible' presented to you post sale.
> **Keep your own copies of your actual replies, just in case.**

♦ The particularly vulnerable part of any change of ownership is the post-sale continuity of trade with clientele. Will customers object to new owners, and move their business elsewhere? Or will they remain loyal to the company and trade with the new owners?

♦ If you know anything that could have influence on these matters, you should declare it as part of your disclosures, but speak to your advisers first.

> **Pay very close attention to disclosures.**
> Disclose everything.
> Ensure that even trivialities are referred to. Better be safe than sorry.

Disclosures are your protection against post sale claims.

But be sensible – some disclosures may discourage buyers.

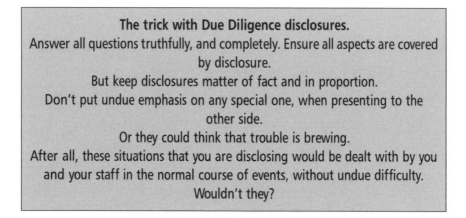

The trick with Due Diligence disclosures.
Answer all questions truthfully, and completely. Ensure all aspects are covered by disclosure.
But keep disclosures matter of fact and in proportion.
Don't put undue emphasis on any special one, when presenting to the other side.
Or they could think that trouble is brewing.
After all, these situations that you are disclosing would be dealt with by you and your staff in the normal course of events, without undue difficulty.
Wouldn't they?

When does due Diligence take place?

The answer to this is 'almost immediately'.

- Interested acquirers/investors will gain 'broad brush' information on your company, before approaching you. Following this, they will ask for your Information Memorandum and possibly organise a flying incognito visit to meet you, and see the company's operations. At this meeting it is probable that preliminary discussions will take place.

- Acquirers/investors wishing to progress further would appoint their own advisers, who will arrange a brief introductory meeting with your advisers. This appointment of their advisers indicates that they are serious, because they are incurring advisers' costs and expenditure.

◆ About now, the acquirer/investor will make a preliminary written offer to you. To go forward to Due Diligence your corporate finance specialists will insist on the acquirer/investor signing a Confidentiality Agreement, and probably Heads of Terms, or Heads of Agreement.

See 'Heads of Terms', Chapter 15.

The scope of Due Diligence

> If you ask any owner manager who has undergone the Due Diligence experience, they will tell you that they have been shocked by the amount and scope of information requested.

There are several broad headings for examination, which we list below. However, in specialist industries there may well be more than listed, all peculiar to the specialism involved. Due Diligence will cover **all aspects** of the company's business.

Pensions Due Diligence

In recent years there has been an explosion in the problems related to pensions, and in particular pension funds that are in fact under-funded. Pensions Due Diligence could be the first of the Due Diligence enquiries to take place. Any further deal discussions may well be contingent on you satisfying acquirers/ investors that the pensions Due Diligence delivers an acceptable level of risk.

Purchasers and investors are cautious of the huge liability that pensions problems can impose. Many recent proposed deals have fallen at this first hurdle.

> In 2005, the Government Pension Regulator acquired the power to demand monies from 'those persons responsible for any under-funded scheme'. If you sell the company with a pension deficit, you and all other related shareholders could be liable as 'connected parties', to make good the deficit.

Any acquirer/investor will be required to file a funding plan covering the next three to five years of that pension scheme, before your deal is allowed to complete.

> So, it is worthwhile setting your pension scheme to rights, well before sale, taking specific specialist advice to do so. Additionally, it is a good idea to involve the Government's Pension Regulator in the sale. If your obligations are fully met, he has the power to issue clearance on the deal. This 'clearance' is a statement made by the regulator that all is in order, and if there are problems post sale you will not be pursued.

Constitutional Due Diligence

The corporate structure of the company, its history, date of incorporation, share capital, plus exact details of shareholders, is the information being sought out.

Buyers will want reassurance that they are dealing with the 'owner', and that **you have the legal right to make decisions, negotiate and sell the company on behalf of all shareholders/ partners**. They will not deal with 'committees' of shareholders or partners. Your shareholder agreement or partnership agreements will prove or disprove ownership details to their satisfaction.

Hard copy evidence of the precise corporate structure of your company is needed for the Due Diligence process, together with Articles of Association and Memorandum of Association, plus all other formal documentation regarding the company's constitution. This will include information on your holding companies, subsidiaries or franchises.

Financial Due Diligence

Financial Due Diligence takes a detailed look at the company's internal financial management. This audit scrutinises annual accounts, balance sheet, management accounts, both currently operating, and those from at least the last three years. Also required will be your current bank statement and budget forecasts for the future. All financial aspects are probed in great detail, looking once again for any matters of risk for the acquirers/investors.

At present, the law does not require all companies to have their annual accounts externally audited. But for any company on the market a 'lack of independent audit' could be viewed with suspicion by purchasers. After all, who is to say that everything is correct and compliant with all legislation? Unaudited accounts would lead to very strong warranties and guarantees being imposed by buyers, even supposing they wish to proceed to completion.

A wiser strategy is to 'invest' in external audit, carried out by reputable accountants during the three years preceding your sale. Comparisons will be made between past years' management account forecasts and the actual results achieved.

Analysts are looking at how accurate you are at forecasting events and sticking to your budgets. After all, you are telling them, by way of budget forecasts within your Information Memorandum, that they can aspire to certain levels of sales and profit. So how accurate are you? Can they be sure to achieve what you predict?

In past times, if your budgets and forecasting have been wildly inaccurate, then it will be necessary to summarise, probably in writing to the Due Diligence auditors, the events or trading climate that took you off track.

> Because you are likely to forget the detail of events as time goes by, we advise you make notes at the end of each trading year, on your attainment or otherwise of budget forecasts. These should be written beside your own copies of sales forecast spreadsheets, and held in your own personal safe-keeping, so that you can produce accurate information if needed at a later date.

Consult your corporate finance specialist before releasing such information to the Due Diligence auditors. He may need to put some 'spin' on the detail.

Financial Due Diligence will also review your debt collection policy, your age of debt, and any factoring or invoice discounting arrangements that are in place.

Similarly, it will be necessary to exhibit your strategy on payment to creditors, stating how many days you take to pay your creditors, plus any special arrangements you may have, say for discounts, rebates, stock holding, 'just in time' delivery or similar.

Considerable significance will be placed on the net and gross profit margins that you claim to be making. If your margins are significantly different from others in the same industry sector, precise explanation of your means of attaining these figures, plus some corroboration, will be requested.

It is true to say that all matters of a financial nature, from employees' salaries, directors' remuneration, company cash investments, debt management, and director loans, and company loans will come under very close scrutiny. This list is by no means exhaustive.

In general terms, the Due Diligence auditors are trying to get a feeling for how the company deals with its financial management. If you can demonstrate meticulous book-keeping, they will feel fairly relaxed about the whole. Their radar is triggered by poor record-keeping, and obvious discrepancies of substantial sums. They are attempting to flush out irregularities, fraud and financial mismanagement that would pose risk for an acquirer.

Tax Due Diligence

No acquirer/investor will wish to be involved in any kind of conflict with VAT or HM Revenue & Customs. Tax irregularities would probably be a deal breaker or, if such problems come to light later, they will have strong post-sale implications for you.
Tax dealings whilst the company is in your ownership are your responsibility. This responsibility **will not** be assumed by new acquirers/investors.

Bearing this in mind, you will be very closely interrogated about all tax matters. The replies will need hard copy corroboration. Interest will be taken in all taxation affairs, covering the last six years (although this may not be exclusive if problems come to light). HM Revenue & Customs is a broad portfolio of all taxes PAYE, VAT, National Insurance, pensions, customs duty, and so on – and will be pertaining to your company, holding company, and any franchises that you operate.

You may be required by buyers to provide a tax 'Deed of

Covenant', which is an indemnity covering all outstanding tax issues. Your auditing accountants will organise this.

Since most dealings with HMRC are conducted in writing, it is sensible to retain copies of all such transactions and letters as they occur, prior to exit. File everything in sensible logical, easily retrievable fashion, which makes life simple in trading and certainly is a bonus at Due Diligence. Retain as much hard copy evidence as possible just in case it is ever needed.

Commercial Due Diligence

Commercial Due Diligence probes all commercial deals, agreements, legal contracts and arrangements that the company has, or once had, in place. Once again, this audit seeks to flush out any risk for the purchaser.

Private equity or other financial equity support deals will be investigated. Although it is likely that such support will dissolve when your company is acquired, the buyers are looking for any risk factors that will arise when the funds are withdrawn. Additionally, they are looking at the terms of your private equity agreement to ensure the company sale will be approved, and without covenants or terms from the private equity becoming enforceable upon new owners.

Loans from all sources will be investigated, together with the terms, conditions and covenants attached to such loans. Buyers are unlikely to take over your loans post sale.

Grants from any source will be scrutinised, once again checking terms, conditions and covenants. It is usual for grants to have to be repaid in full if the company is sold to a new owner. This would usually take place at the same time as the sale completion, so that funds can be taken straight out of sale proceeds and transferred to the grantor.

Your industry accreditations will be checked out for risk factors. It will be particularly important to buyers to ensure that the accreditation may be assigned to the new owner post sale. Check out your accreditation expiry dates. It is preferable to a buyer that accreditations have a long period to run after your exit. If not, then discussions and re-appraisal may be necessary with the accreditation panel.

P/E ratio may well be affected by the accreditation status.

Due Diligence auditors will check out all leases, contracts, arrangements, or formal legal agreements to discover cancellation clauses and penalties for cancellation, etc. It is quite normal for trading companies to hold all manner of trading contracts, leases and agreements. But if the acquirer/investor decides to cancel these post acquisition, he will not wish to encounter unduly long or expensive cancellation penalties. If these clauses and covenants can't be overcome, this would be reflected in the price paid for your company. It is just possible that you may have to change the terms and conditions of some of these arrangements to fit in with your exit plans.

> In making such alterations remember that there is still need for secrecy. Do not reveal that you intend to exit.

Broadly speaking the company's contractual matters fall into the following categories:

- Those that are considered as **customers** of the company.

- Those that are considered **suppliers** to the company.

- Those related to **staff employment**.

- Those related to **property**.

- Those related to **company financial support**.

- Those related to **franchise dealings** or similar.

Contracts, agreements, rental agreements and other arrangements with customers

> Customer contract expiry dates is a factor that will invite very close audit inspection from your buyers.

Due Diligence auditors will be checking out customer contracts to ensure that expiry dates run a good way into the future to produce a forthcoming revenue stream. Contract expiry dates that are staggered, not all occurring together, is preferred.

These auditors are looking for risks for the buyers, such as the contracts not being assignable, or even containing prohibitive or expensive covenants and clauses. They are also looking out for contracts that automatically terminate upon sale of the company, or are not novatable to an acquirer.

Contracts with clients, especially those running into future years, should contain clauses that give the opportunity to increase prices in line with inflation. It should also be possible under the terms to impose or negotiate surcharges in the event of excessive and unforeseen national or global fuel, materials, labour or other price increases. Thus the contract will still be profitable in future years, for yourself or new owners, despite inflation and unforeseen price increases.

Buyers will wish to see each individual customer's actual contract terms and conditions. They will scrutinise terms relating to cancellation should the buyer decide to terminate with the customer, or vice versa. Auditors will be looking for the cost and penalties involved in such action.

Contracts, agreements, rental agreements and other arrangements with suppliers

Acquirers/investors will be looking for flexibility in any contracts with suppliers.

Acquirers/investors may wish to continue with the current supply arrangements or to increase the business with your suppliers. They may alternatively wish to cancel the contract, in order to be supplied by another company. Any supplier contract that is to run for too long into the future, or has extremely expensive cancellation penalties, may have an adverse impact on the price paid for the company especially if it is non negotiable.

Price rises, inflation busting increases, materials change, or unforeseen circumstance will all be important to an acquirer/ investor. These terms may give a supplier opportunity to increase his prices, which is not desirable. So it would be important to see terms built into the contract allowing for renegotiation.

Due Diligence auditors will be looking out for contracts that are or are not transferable, and the terms of any transfer. Auditors are also looking for terms that are non negotiable. Always build negotiability into your contracts. The politics of being supplied by particular named companies may or may not be important to your acquirer/investor. If you hold contracts with penalties, and no opportunity to cancel or change the terms, these will be flushed out. **P/E ratio could be adversely affected**.

Due Diligence regarding property contracts and agreements

All property leases, agreements, contract arrangements concerning property you own or occupy must be available for scrutiny, together with copies for the auditors to keep.

Property that you own, whether it is currently occupied by you or others, that will form part of the exit sale, must be declared together with all of its documentation. If the property is rented out by you then the tenancy agreements must also be available for scrutiny and be copied to the auditors. These will be examined, looking for terms that would 'lock in' the new owners, or have unwelcome covenants and/or penalties.

If your limited company operates from rented accommodation, then the lease is probably in the name of your company. Buyers will wish to scrutinise the lease looking for the length of the lease, and terms that allow re-assignment of the lease.

New owners may wish to move your operation to a different site, thus vacating your building. It will be important to know whether they can reassign the lease, or sub-let the building. Leases of property will be examined to see if they are 'Continuing Liability' lease, or 'Guarantor Liability', or if the lease utilises the 'rent deposit' scheme. This will form part of your negotiating stance.

Property Due Diligence will also cover maintenance contracts that are held with suppliers to the property, for: garden and grounds maintenance; pest control; air conditioning maintenance; drinking water suppliers; contract cleaners; hygiene services; window cleaners; and so on. All of these contracts must be available to view. Copies of current copies will be requested. Once again, freedom to cancel contracts, cancellation clauses, penalties and associated costs are all being evaluated.

Disclosure is necessary if there are any known plans for compulsory purchase or similar. Property owned and part of the exit sale will be independently valued by independent property valuers. You will pay for this valuation.

Due Diligence audit on franchise arrangements

These will be subjected to endless Due Diligence questioning. All of the negotiated terms, history of the franchisee's compliance with the terms and conditions will be requested, together with hard copy evidence.

- Property ownership or leases will form a major part of the enquiry.

- The terms of business between the franchisee and yourself will be interrogated, looking for unwelcome obligation to your acquirer/investor.

- Items of equipment of major significance will be probed regarding precise ownership, leases, maintenance contracts and relevant cancellation penalties or covenants.

- All documents, past, present or future, will be endlessly examined, seeking risk or unwelcome obligation for new owners, as well as advantage for them.

Commercial Due Diligence results

Having gained what they believe to be sufficient information on commercial Due Diligence, acquirers/investors will be in a position to consider:

- Synergies between the buyer's existing operation(s).

- Business opportunities that may exist for customer base expansion, company growth, operational improvements, cost reductions.

- The sustainability of your cash flow.

- What's in it for the acquirer/investor?

- Acquirers wishing to merge your company with another that they own will need to consider a company integration plan, using data gathered.

Commercial Due Diligence can prove a valuable influencer on the P/E ratio.

Intellectual assets Due Diligence

This audit offers you the opportunity to demonstrate and give proof that:

◆ The company's intellectual property is as valuable as predicted in the Information Memorandum, and will live up to expectations.

◆ Brands are strong enough to live on through a change of ownership without loss of trade.

◆ The brand or intellectual property has already attained a certain percentage market penetration, leaving future percentage for buyers to develop. (Or is the market for the product over-supplied?)

All patents or patents pending documentation will be needed for verification and must be passed over at completion. Additionally required will be documentation in detail on trade marks, design, copyright registrations, branding, accreditations and domain names. Included in this sector would be any contract arrangements that cover the 'sole supplier' basis that may exist for products, or licence to sell in certain geographical areas.
All documentation on any product that you claim exclusivity over will be requested.
Consult your corporate finance specialist before exhibiting the above. They will advise on how much and in what format this sensitive data is exhibited.

From the information obtained a buyer can determine:

◆ Whether the projections for future business returns, related to intellectual assets, are realistic and obtainable by a new owner.

◆ Whether the company really does have future potential for success via its intellectual assets.

◆ The auditors are seeking any patent infringements and illegal use that could lead to litigation. Pending litigation will also be uncovered by this audit, and will discourage buyers.

Sales and marketing Due Diligence

The sales and marketing Due Diligence that you undergo will look into all the methods and facts connected to the company's trading operations. This will cover customers, the turnover generated, plus the products/services that are being sold, and the precise method of selling and delivering those goods/services.

The auditors will examine:

◆ The number of customers and the spread of business across those customers. If it seems that the majority of the company's trade is with one client or a very limited number, there is a risk factor here (suppose you lost that client).

◆ Actual individual and average customer spend per annum, over each of the last three years and in this current year to date, will be scrutinised. Trends upwards or downwards are being exposed.

◆ Any seasonal factors must be explained fully, and budget forecasts explained to show how and when compensation is made.

> All manner and type of sales analysis will be requested.

◆ Lists of names and addresses of your clientele, especially those that are of significant turnover, will be requested. Take advice from your corporate finance specialist on revealing this sensitive data. Auditors want to see if the prospective acquirers/ investors already trade with these clients anyway. Also they are investigating whether these 'customers of significance' will transfer their business to your acquirers/investors post sale.

◆ Your company's methods of selling to your clients will be closely questioned, alongside the commission and overrides paid to sales people.

◆ Your marketing plans, the effectiveness of these marketing strategies, together with associated costs will be queried. Where brand management or product placement is involved the questions will be particularly probing.

◆ Future order books, contracts into the future, will require verification. Auditors are looking to see what business is certain to come their way post sale. They wish to see if there are any unwelcome conditions attached to these sales orders and the anticipated dates of these orders.

◆ Comparisons of your marketing strategies with those of your direct competitors will be made.

◆ Information on trade competitors, both opinion and published proof of who they are and their status in the market. Alongside this, they want proof of your company's market penetration, compared with the competitors' market penetration.

Information on your competitors' activities and their marketing ploys compared with your own company will be requested. As well as this, any indirect competition should be revealed, so that buyers can gauge your position in the marketplace.
Publicity via magazine articles and industry data can suffice to corroborate your opinion. Make this part of your preparations for sale.

Of late, another factor that could be of interest, depending on your business activity, is the danger of threats to your business from terrorism. Sadly these days this is a feature of some risk. Is your business likely to suffer from demonstration by 'activists'? If your business is in some way linked to travel, you could suffer loss of trade from aeroplane terrorists and so on. **These risk factors would be reflected in your P/E ratio**.

Technology Due Diligence

There are two main purposes to this investigation.

Firstly, it is essential to identify all technologies within your company, and establish that they are compliant in all legislative matters, holding full and appropriate licences, plus written permissions to use the applications, etc.

Secondly, auditors will look at your manufacturing technologies used in producing the company' products/services. Points to consider are the post-sale operation of these technologies. Will they be adequate for additional volume? Will the technology integrate into the new owner's schemes? How will operators feel about change of owners? Does this hold significance?

The auditors will scrutinise your technology, asking:

- Does it live up to its promise?

- Does it require specialist handling (in other words, will it only work if the currently employed employees go with it?)

- Has it been fully tested?

- Is it foolproof?

- Are there future pitfalls awaiting a new owner?

- Is it up to the minute or old fashioned and needing repair or replacement?

- Have all patents, design rights, etc., been applied for to cover your invention? Or is there someone out there already copying your idea?

The investigation of technology Due Diligence may use the services of specialists in this field. Once again, technology Due Diligence is searching out risk factors.

Legal Due Diligence

This investigation is also looking for risk factors, but this time it seeks to protect the acquirer/investor from claims from past irregularities and pending litigation. Areas of investigation will cover both the company's background and that of the principal officers. The areas that will be probed are:

- Criminal records, plus association with the criminal fraternity.

- Violations of the law, disciplinary procedures, or disregard of company law.

- Litigation, bankruptcy, financial irregularity.

- County court judgements, unpaid fines or taxes.

- Credit or financial problems.

- Debt, and past business failures.

- Fraudulent credentials, misrepresentation.

- Poor reputation. Both the company reputation and that of the principals is an oft overlooked feature, yet is critically important. No one likes to deal with someone they don't trust.

◆ Any other legal wrongdoing.

In addition to this, the audit will endeavour to discover:

◆ That all past and current Statutory Registers and returns to Companies House and other government authorities are up to date and fully submitted.

◆ That the company is and has in the past operated within all laws, including company law.

◆ Whether the marital status of the owners is of consequence, because any marital breakdown can have implications on the ownership and future of the business.

Environmental Due Diligence

Yet again acquirers/investors' auditors are evaluating risk potential. Environmental issues have a nasty habit of turning up out of the blue, and becoming expensive. The investigation will examine property matters, maintenance, and compliance with all waste regulations, pollutants, fire regulation, plus all environmental laws.

Your properties will no doubt have undergone many and various inspections. Assuming everything has passed the various authorities' inspection, full certificates of compliance will have been issued. It is these that are so valuable in the Due Diligence process and need to be exhibited.

Contracts that you have with pest control companies, air condition servicing, drinking water cleansing, inspection and testing by the water authority, plus other similar services should all be available for the auditors' inspection.

> Buildings situated on old, untidy and overgrown sites may give cause for a buyer's concern, especially in connection with invasive plants (such as knotweed) and pollution of the ground from old workings.
> Where this is likely, a site review may be conducted by experts, who would be invited to produce an environmental assessment, including advice on 'clean up'. You would pay for this inspection. You would also be invited to fund 'clean up', or face a sales proceeds reduction.

Information technology Due Diligence

There is no doubt that this audit will be conducted by computer 'techy' people. They will evaluate the performance of the company's hardware and software in the light of future integration with the buyer's system.

- Under investigation also will be your IT management, their capabilities, and loyalty.

- Concerning your IT staff, will it be essential to retain their services to run your IT system? Or will the buyer's own 'techy' people be able to run your system?

- Auditors will look for software licences on your system and all of its applications being up to date. They are looking for patent or licence infringement and any litigation pending.

- Your computer systems will be evaluated as a company asset.

Employment Due Diligence

Employment Due Diligence is seeking to evaluate any risk factors connected with the employees of your company, especially and in particular any ongoing, past, or anticipated future industrial tribunals or litigation.

The audit will delve into details of employees both current and those employed over the last five years. Job application forms, contracts of employment, work appraisals, employee history, absenteeism, maternity/paternity and other pertinent information will need to be documented. You will also have to produce employees' 'reasons for leaving' and the address of their next employer.

Staff employment contracts

Copies of all staff and director contracts will need to be exhibited to the Due Diligence auditors. They are looking for terms that have been negotiated and written down that operate into the future, which is post sale, together with compliance with employment law.

Any terms of payment or payment in kind to staff and directors, in lieu of notice, will be especially closely examined. These may be evaluated and could be deducted from the sale proceeds if they seem especially significant.

Past employment problems, and any possibilities of future problems occurring, must be declared in 'disclosures' if they are known to you (or if you have even the slightest suspicion that there could be a 'situation'). This will avoid post-sale repercussions.

You will even be asked to provide lists of people who came for interviews, together with the reasons why they did not become an employee. Hard copy verification of all facts (even interviewees) will be required. The auditors are looking for possibilities of litigation.

Any employment changes, wage increases (apart from annual increments), negotiated with staff during company sale negotiations will be viewed very sceptically.

Key personnel
Part of employment Due Diligence is an assessment of staff employed in significant roles at the time of sale, in order that the acquirers/investors can produce a post-sale integration plan. Therefore you will need to produce comprehensive information on these key personnel. The usual risk factors of litigation and tribunal are also being sought out.

♦ Key personnel are easily identified as staff on whom you are personally reliant. They may well form part of your Executive Team, and be running the company whilst you are dealing with the sale. Their personal details, by way of a CV plus information on their experience, knowledge, relationships with other staff, and clients/suppliers, together with the level of authority that they have been allowed to hold, should be prepared for release to auditors.

♦ Due Diligence auditors will want to know and understand the reasons why these people are key members of your staff. What do they do and how do they accomplish it that makes them so important to the running of the company? This information should be included in the CV of each individual.

- A staff organisation chart is often requested detailing the key personnel, plus a 'who reports to whom' detail.

- Comprehensive details on their remuneration structure, to include bonuses, incentives, company vehicles or expense account and any forward payment promises, together with their contract of employment, will need to be divulged.

- Any compensatory payment schemes in lieu of notice should new owners decide not to employ these personnel will be closely scrutinised. If they seem particularly expensive this could deter buyers. Alternatively, the amount could be deducted from the sale price.

Other Due Diligence investigations

Being the 'protection' factor for acquirers/investors they will feel that

there are no areas that cannot be investigated.

Following any company acquisition there will always be things that crop up after the deal. But if you have covered these in your disclosures, then you have given the acquirer/investor advance warning of possible difficulties ahead and thus can't be asked for compensation post sale.

Prepare in advance

So now you have a good idea of the process and the questions you may well be asked. You will find that answering Due Diligence 'on the hoof', plus producing corroborative evidence, is tricky and nerve wracking, and could cause an expensive complication if handled incorrectly.

The answer is pre-sale preparations. Indeed, preparations made as the company is evolving and growing are best – managing the data to become orderly, by retaining copies and filing logically. Develop a simplified system of record-keeping that is adhered to rigorously by all staff.

Example

A typical question that may be asked is 'How many jobs were filled, and who were the people employed, and who has left, within the last five years? And why did they leave?'

Discovering the answer to this question can be done without any undue problem, if you operate a simplified system such as this:

- File the advertisement inviting staff to apply for a particular job. (Write the date on it.)

- File all successful and unsuccessful applicants' reply forms. Write on the form the reason for not offering the applicant the post in question. Be careful not to allude to race, religion, colour, creed, age, or other 'non politically correct' comments. Even job applicants have rights.

- File in date, or some other logical order, for easy retrieval. Alphabetical is not usually to be recommended for this since you may not remember their names in say five years' time. Dated recording is better.

- File the 'new starters' personnel form with a copy of their reply to your advert. New starters form should show past employment, full health information, etc. Complete the new employee's starting date on form, name of job taken up, and starting salary. Should the person leave, record the date and reason for leaving. Keep sensibly and logically filed. It is then easy to go back over old staff leavers.

♦ All employees should have their own file, with contracts of employment, promotions, discipline matters, etc, recorded within.

♦ Contracts, legal documents, etc, should all be sensibly filed under easily retrieved headings.

♦ As information ages, file in archives in date order. It will be easy to store archived files within a designated storage area, retrieval being easy if they are marked with the date.

Adopt this kind of approach to all matters. Careful filing, without loss, is the key to Due Diligence preparation. Add to this the ability to interrogate your computer records via print out reports, and you will find it is not such a horrendous task as it first seems.

CHAPTER SEVENTEEN

Completion Day

In this chapter:

- *Who attends?*
- *What happens?*
- *Transfer of funds*
- *Distribution of sales receipts*
- *Escrow accounts*
- *Release of escrow accounts*
- *Baskets (de minimis)*
- *Electronic completion*

Who attends?

At last you arrive at completion day (commonly called Completion). The venue will be spacious, to cater for you, your company secretary, your corporate lawyers plus their team; perhaps your auditing accountants, your corporate finance specialists, possibly your bank, maybe your private equity or angels team, and probably also the shareholders.

Your buyers similarly number a large group: the buyers' principal, legal team, accountants' team, bankers, financial backers.

You will be escorted by your lawyers, and surrounded by your team of advisers.

Events of the day are orchestrated by the lawyers of the buyers.

Frenetic energy and organised chaos seem to rule the day.

Let your lawyers guide you.

Now you know why you need competent, experienced corporate lawyers.

What happens?

It is at Completion that all documents and money will be exchanged, thus transferring ownership of your company to the purchasers.

Your lawyers will have presented you with a catalogue of essential documents to bring to the meeting:

◆ Share certificates
◆ Originals of Memorandum of Association
◆ Originals of Articles of Association
◆ Company cheque book(s)
◆ Company minute book
◆ Shareholder agreements
◆ Deeds
◆ Documentation re trade marks, patents, licences, franchise agreements
◆ Company seal
◆ Bank mandates
◆ Tax records
◆ Share option agreements
◆ Securities
◆ Statutory books, registers

There will be many other documents particular to your company.

During the course of the day, your lawyers will guide you through an abundance of signings of shareholder meetings and director meetings, concerned with the resignation of one set of directors, company secretary and auditors and the appointment of another set.

There will be changes of registered office addresses, bank mandates, and the sale and purchase agreement. According to the size and type of deal, together with the date (which in some cases is significant), a whole host of documents are required to 'complete' the sale transaction. Don't worry. It all seems to go on around you . . . your lawyers will be in control.

> ### Practice Completion. . .the dress rehearsal
> Some days before completion you will have been through a sort of 'dress rehearsal'. All of the paperwork concerned with completion itself will have been examined by yourselves, together with your lawyers. These documents will have been scrutinised in the finest detail, making alterations as necessary, so that inaccuracies are addressed and corrected as you go along.
> The sale and purchase agreement will have been drafted and redrafted many times, as the professionals negotiate on your behalf, and hold discussions with you and your whole professional team, to arrive at acceptable wording.
> You should check out Disclosures with a fine tooth comb, looking for mistakes or imperfections. Think carefully over your business affairs to see that everything which could need explanation at a later date is covered by a disclosure.

Beware . . .Things can still go awry even at Completion. Even though you have arrived finally at Completion, situations can arise and at the very last moment completion fails.

An air of suspicion hangs over the lawyers, who seem to trust nobody. A casual or inopportune remark from you can raise doubts in the buyers' mind. So be discreet and quiet. Ensure that you have brought with you **all documents and items**, as instructed by lawyers. Omissions or items forgotten can have serious repercussions, even failure to complete. Check over all aspects of the paperwork and items in good time beforehand, ensuring their ready availability for this day.

Transfer of funds

Prior to completion day, your advisers will have checked that your buyers have sufficient funds available to complete the deal. They will have prepared banks and financiers for today's events, so that when professionals on all sides are happy, the transfer of these funds will be initiated.

These days this takes place electronically, often causing some nail biting on both sides until funds reach their destination. But eventually there will be a moment of confirmation that all has occurred as planned.

It is usual for funds and loan notes to transfer into the **purchasers' lawyer's** bank for safekeeping, awaiting distribution.

Distribution of sales receipts

Following Completion, the funds from the sale are transferred to **your lawyer's** bank minus any escrow account funds. Lawyers preside over release of the funds.

Your advisers will have prepared their bills in advance of completion day, which they present to you privately, for approval.

Lawyers will deduct collectively all professional fees, with which they pay the various agencies involved. These are re-charged out proportionately to each shareholder, according to their percentage shareholding, and deducted accordingly from their proceeds.

The purchasing lawyers retain in their bank the entire escrow sum, awaiting distribution at a predetermined later date, as appropriate. Following Completion your lawyers will release to shareholders their percentage cash sums (minus escrow accounts and any other costs).

Escrow accounts

You will not be surprised that purchasers are frequently reluctant to pay out the entire agreed sale price in one single payment. They want to be assured that the Due Diligence process was accurate and honestly completed, and that they have not been misled. Thus a previously agreed percentage of the sales proceeds is retained by the purchasers' lawyers for an agreed time span, or until the purchaser is happy with the results of his purchase or investment. This is called the **escrow account.** Funds held in this escrow account are sums negotiated between vendor and purchaser.

Where a purchaser perceives risk is a likely possibility with this acquisition, he will negotiate strong, long and expensive warranty clauses, which will be held over in the escrow account.

> It has not been unheard of for the whole of the sale proceeds to be held back. And it has also been heard of for the escrow account to be 'on hold' for up to three years.

This is where the reputation of yourself and your company can be an influential factor. Poor reputation may lead to long expensive warranties that translate into money held over in the escrow account. This could also be the case if your annual accounts have not been independently audited by a reputable accountancy practice. Or if there is a hint of an asset shortfall or some other suspicious circumstance. Indeed, any risk factors could be covered by this method of retaining some or the entire negotiated sale price until it is proven that the deal is free of problem.

Release of escrow accounts

If the buyer makes successful claims on the escrow account, it will compensate the buyer accordingly, thus reducing the vendor's sale consideration. If no claims are made, the escrow account will be released at the negotiated time, in full.

Eventually, as time passes, the escrow account will be released to the vendor, minus any compensation. Having received the funds from the buyer's solicitors, the distribution will be made by your lawyers to each shareholder, according to their percentage shareholding. Thus no single shareholder is penalised by reduced funds. Everyone is proportionately penalised according to their % shareholding.

Escrow accounts should attract interest rates which at least equate to building society interest rates, whilst in the holding of the lawyers. Your lawyers will negotiate this prior to completion. This sum could be quite large so it should not be overlooked. Your lawyers are under a professional obligation to do this on your behalf, although occasionally they forget to pay out at the due date. Jog their memory.

Baskets (de minimis)

It would be rare for the purchase of a company to be completely free of repercussion.

It is annoying to a buyer if these repercussions lead to some loss of his invested money. Equally, it would be annoying to the vendor and could prove expensive if the purchaser were to keep making trivial claims for trifling amounts against the escrow account.

So a method of dealing with this is negotiated, whereby claims must aggregate to a prearranged set figure, before triggering a claim against the escrow account. This is commonly called 'Baskets'. Your professionals will negotiate this on your behalf at the sale and purchase agreement compilation.

Electronic completion

In these days of hectic living it may be necessary to 'complete' the sale and purchase process by electronic means, using fax, e-mails, internet, post, couriers, and phones, especially conference phones, and video links.

Where this is the likely method of completion, the professionals from both sides will have agreed and organised the methodology, the circulation of documents, and the timing of proceedings.

In this case, following the exchange of documents and signatures, you will finally get a phone call to say that funds have transferred and the sale is now complete. It is only at this stage that you can tell the workforce, in the prearranged manner.

Even when using electronic completion, the escrow account and funds distribution by lawyers remain the same as described earlier.

Electronic completion is far less of an event than the meeting of all concerned, but where arranged professionally it is just as legal.

CHAPTER EIGHTEEN

Post Completion

In this chapter:

- *At last...*
- *Investments*
- *Security*
- *Time to smell the roses*

At last...

You have made it. Completion day over, funds have arrived at your bank. Now is the time to get on with your life's plans.

But all this personal wealth has put you on the radar of HMRC. So here are some worthwhile tips.

- Keep accurate records on exactly how much, on what date, and in what format you received the sales revenue from the company sale. By that we mean did you receive shares, cash, car, other payment.

- Are there any periphery costs? Dinners with advisers, gifts, how much and to whom? etc.

It is really important to retain this information for your own eyes, because you will certainly forget some of the detail in the post-sale euphoria. And at some time in the future you will need it!

> **Keep private records** throughout this next era of your life, detailing gifts, to whom, dates and amounts and for what purpose was the gift made. This information will be useful in verifying income tax.

◆ You should also record high value personal expenditure, not forgetting records on how much tax you paid, the amount, and when paid. It may be useful to retain a copy of the tax demand.

◆ HMRC can go back over your financial status for the last six years, and further if they believe there may be irregularities. A Revenue investigation is to be avoided at all costs. It is seriously disruptive and nerve-wracking. Retain all documentation regarding the company sale, to be on the safe side.

◆ Appoint an independent accountant who is expert in tax matters. This is worthwhile, to complete tax returns and to stand between you and the Revenue man in case of an investigation or queries.

Investments

Many owner managers will be uncertain about how to invest this vast wealth that has now come their way.

> **So take your time**.
> Put the capital in a high interest easy access deposit account while you decide on a reliable, honest financial adviser.

In selecting this adviser try the beauty parade technique. Some will offer to charge for their services. Others will take their fee out of your investment plan. Which is best in each circumstance?

But before you lock your capital away think carefully about what *you* want to do with your life.

Consider inheritance tax. And remember that HMRC are expecting their share of your wealth, both now and for some time to come.

Ask advisers about the best available, low risk, investments that will bring tax-free monthly income. This is an ever changing scenario, as the country and global finance flow, and governments seek to take a share of your hard earned cash.

Security

Sadly there are always those people who would like to part you from your wealth, either by theft, or deception. And while it is a natural wish to shout from the rooftops that you are now rich, resist the temptation. Even casual conversations can be a security risk.

And there are always those people who are jealous of success, and would seek to ruin your happiness in your achievements. So it is back to the world of secrecy once more. You will be used to this by now.

Time to smell the roses

Take the time to enjoy your life from now on.

You have worked for it.

Appendix

- *Management accounts explained*
- *Calculate your age of debt*
- *Sample monthly management report*
- *Cash flow forecast*
- *Setting a budget*
- *Budget report*
- *Information memorandum*

Management accounts explained

What are management accounts?

Allowing your business to run on day by day, month after month, with no structured plan of action or record as to what has happened is poor management that will eventually result in ruin.

Much better to plan ahead, set budget predictions for monthly sales figures, and record the results achieved. This is the way you will find out the nuances of your business, and be totally in control.

Some useful records are included in this Appendix, so that you can see the layout. Definitely to be recommended are:

- sales budget predictions
- actual sales results achieved
- cash flow report
- age of debt report
- costs of sales
- costs of running the company, all departments.

If you employ a qualified management accountant he will be familiar with all of this. **Acquirers/investors will expect to see these records for the past three years.**

Calculate your age of debt (or debtor collection period)

Knowing how long it takes to collect your outstanding debt from customers is key to good financial management. Attention to this will repay you, by the need to borrow less cash to continue in business.

Calculation:
Divide the amount owed by customers by the annual sales turnover and multiply by 365.

Amount owed by debtors	£30,000
Divide by credit sales	£250,000 × 365 = (43.8) **44 days**

This indicates that it takes an average of 44 days from invoice date to receipt of payment. A very good collection average is about 55 days.

Retail will be 0 (nil) days where goods are paid for in cash only over the counter at purchase. Many companies have 60 days debtor collection period. What is your industry average?

Setting a budget

What is a budget?

You will find your English dictionary explains the word 'budget' as 'the amount of money needed or available'.

In running your business it is of prime concern to the management to know how much money is needed so that commitments can be met, and it is of equal importance to know how much money is available. And naturally you want to know how much profit you can create via your sales to meet your obligations. So the budget becomes a plan of the future business activities to create money and also a plan of how all available monies will be spent in achieving those sales results that you would like to see.

It is customary to set a fairly detailed budget (or plan) for the coming

Monthly Management Accounts Report

	1	2	3	4	5	6	7	8	9	10	11	12	Total
Sales	55,000												
Cost of sales	35,200												
Contribution	19,800												
Gross profit %	36%												
Overheads													
Sales	4,060												
Warehouse	2,790												
Administration	2,200												
Computer	1,500												
General management	3,200												
Total overheads	13,750												
Operating profit	6,050												
%	11%												
Finance charges	1,100												
Net profit before tax	4,950												
Net profit %	9												

This spreadsheet shows the actual results obtained in one month of a 12-month year. No doubt you could devise a similar reporting system for your company. It is sensible to use this same spreadsheet format to show your budget predictions for your forthcoming year.

Cash Flow Report

	1	2	3	4	5	6	7	8	9	10	11	12	Total
Opening balance	−15,613												
Income													
Customers	56,823												
Others	5,000												
Total available	46,210												
Expenditure													
Suppliers	4,844												
Wages	33,688												
VAT													
Repayment finance	20,000												
Capital expenditure													
Total expenditure	58,532												

Explanation

This is the beginning of a typical report. No doubt your accountant will produce something similar that depicts either the 12 months or 13 months of your year. Using this report also for weekly/monthly/annual cash flow records you can keep track of your funds. You will also be able to see any shortfall up ahead, and so do something about it. Naturally you will complete the column entries as they apply to your company.

next financial year, and to cover a complete year's business, in the budget.

Your budget should set target figures for sales turnover, which in turn shows the expenditure generated for all of the other departments.

The reasons you should set a budget

Allowing any business to run on day after day, month after month, year after year with no plan of what may happen is clearly poor management.

It is so much safer to plan for developments, to know 'where you are going', and the timescales involved in attaining the goals being set. In setting the budget one can see financial opportunities arising or, conversely, financial pitfalls or reasons for caution. All of this allows you to manage the business efficiently and properly.

What will you gain from budget setting?

The process involved entails close examination of all aspects of the business as it is today.

Using information taken from current performance, it is possible to project results for next financial year. Thus critical analysis of current trading will show current weaknesses, which will need correction, and conversely highlight strengths that could be developed. Any new ideas can readily be evaluated hypothetically to see if they can be incorporated into the business and, if so, the timing of the incorporation can be seen.

This is the time when good managers can see what is **really happening** to their business. Both short- and long-term plans can be made. This is a useful time to examine SWOT – strengths, weaknesses, opportunities, threats – and then **plan** appropriate action.

When to set a budget

Traditionally, and usefully, your work on setting a new budget should take place just prior to the start of a new financial year.

The completed copies should be questioned, amended, then approved by the board of directors (where applicable) in sufficient time for the company managers to begin to take preliminary steps, so that on day one of the new financial year managers will hit the ground running. Any preparations will have already taken place (for instance, additional staff engaged, or new machinery purchased).

Rebudgeting should take place during the course of a year if it is obvious that the original budget is not working satisfactorily, or if a set of unforeseen circumstances have had good/adverse impact. This will take account of all new factors, to present a more realistic set of figures, to work towards.

How you begin to set a budget

So that you can predict the future **accurately** it is essential to have available all facts concerning all aspects of the business as it is today. Only when you know what is actually happening, as opposed to what you think is happening, can you go forward. Listed are some of the areas which should be examined in detail:

- Monthly sales turnover. Are your markets good enough and is your product range strong enough to be developed?
- Cost of producing goods. How do you deal with 'wastage' in the manufacturing process?
- Overheads should be examined minutely, even down to how many letters are sent and the cost of the postage. Very close examination of 'age of debt' (the length of time it takes clients to pay). Slow payers and bad debts should be examined and a strategy for management implemented firmly and speedily.
- Are delivery arrangements acceptable, speedy, inexpensive, and traceable?
- Where can you eliminate unnecessary expense, without the business suffering?
- How can you increase turnover? New markets, new products, better sales staff, and better sales promotions. Are you employing too many or too few staff?

Budget Report

Months	1	2	3	4	5
Sales	15,000	15,000	16,000	16,500	16,500
Product A	7,600	7,600	8,200	8,300	8,300
Product B	4,200	4,200	5,000	5,800	5,800
Product C	3,200	3,200	2,800	2,400	2,400

Budget report showing sales predictions for a 12-month year.
Note periods 6 and 12 total values show low numbers because of seasonal factors.
Different products have different seasonal factors, which show in the peaks and troughs of sales.

♦ Are you spending on marketing without resultant sales turnover? Can it be eliminated, bettered, followed up in a definite manner?

♦ Are financial repayments being kept up to date? Where a loan has been undertaken by the company, is the best use being made of that capital? Or is it being frittered away? Future lenders will look closely at this, before offering a loan.

♦ Have you kept to the original budget which was prepared when applying for a loan? If not, why not?

♦ Are your customers happy? Enough to give repeat business and referrals?

♦ Take into account all factors, and then plan a realistic strategy of development for next year with an eye on what could happen in the year(s) following.

♦ Are there seasonal factors to your business? For instance, how does Christmas affect your sales? Or summer holidays?

♦ Identify the times that are seasonally affected. Consult next year's calendar to see the precise dates. How many days does the Christmas period affect? And so on.

♦ Knowing these factors you can build in an allowance for this next year.

Now you are ready to start the actual budgeting

Look back at last year and previous years.

6	7	8	9	10	11	12	Total
7,000	16,700	17,000	17,500	17,500	18,000	7,000	179,700
3,200	8,400	9,000	9,200	9,500	10,000	3,200	92,500
1,500	6,000	6,500	6,600	7,000	7,000	1,500	61,100
2,300	2,300	1,500	1,700	1,000	1,000	2,300	26,100

- What percentage sales increase is possible next year?
- How would you achieve that increase? Would it be new products, different and wider marketplaces, to expand geographically, take on more sales staff, or what? Work this out manually, giving thought to how it can be achieved, what needs to be provided, or done beforehand to reach those targets. How much extra will it cost? Is it possible?
- Analyse your sales projections product by product. Can you sell more X product or is it easier/better to sell Y product? Then set out your ideas in the form of a spreadsheet.
- Costs should also be set out as a spreadsheet.

You and fellow directors should then see if all of this is possible. If not, then amendments should be made.

You should only produce budgets that are possible. Better to overshoot, rather than **never** reach the target.

Information memorandum

What is the information memorandum?
This is a prospectus prepared by your corporate finance specialists, with your assistance. It is designed to tell all prospective buyers the

information that they will wish to know before deciding whether they are interested in purchase or not. Needless to say this should present a positive spin on your company, and be presented professionally because it needs to stand out from any others they may be considering. Your corporate finance specialist will know what will be the most impressive facts.

The prospectus should be attractive, eye-catching, full of easily read data, and written to be read within 15 to 20 minutes.

Contents
- Introduction.
- Executive summary describing:
  - opportunity being presented
  - background of the company
  - products and services the company supplies
  - strengths of the company
  - reasons for sale.
- History of the company and its ownership.
- Market analysis.
- In-depth products and services.
- Sales and marketing methods.
- Competitive analysis.
- Operation and premises.
- Employees and managers.
- Information systems.
- Financial data.
- Accreditations.
- Corporate brochures that you would normally use in selling your products.
- Location, site plans, maps, photos.
- Press articles.
- Major items of equipment, or significance.

By providing preliminary information, anyone who wishes to pursue this opportunity will make contact to take matters further.

Glossary

Accreditation Officially recognised standards for businesses. These are awarded by government bodies, international councils, or even industry bodies that have their own schemes and regulations which, with satisfactory compliance, will award accreditations.

Acquisition The process whereby one company takes over ownership of another.

Age of debt (or debtor collection period) A table in which the time taken by all the company debtors to pay up is averaged to produce company average number of days.

AIM (Alternative Investment Market) Similar to the Stock Exchange, but with less regulation and geared to smaller companies.

Angels (business angels) Private individuals who invest capital into companies.

Basket (de minimis) Following completion any claims made by the purchaser against the vendor should not be trivial, and are thus aggregated to a set predetermined figure before submission as a claim.

BIMBO (Buy In Management Buy Out) This is a combination of an MBI and MBO. *See MBI and MBO.*

Brand An identifiable mark or name used in association with a company or product.

Budget Chart calculations predicting company income and expenditure.

Budgetary control The process of comparing actual results against budget forecast results.

Business activity The type of work which the business undertakes.

Cash flow Traceability of cash coming into, outward and retained by the company.

CBI Confederation of British Industry.

Consideration The figure that you will receive upon selling the company. This can be a mixture of cash, loan notes, shares, etc.

Continuing liability When you assign your lease to another party you remain liable for payments or terms if they default.

Contribution The difference between the 'buy in' price and the 'selling out' price of a company's goods or services.

Credit control Debt collection and checking credit ratings.

Depreciation Assets which reduce in value over a period of time are said to depreciate. Thus depreciation is a measurement of this reduction in value.

Directors without shareholding Company directors who do not own shares in the company.

Disclosures Statements made by company owners guaranteeing various facts of the business.

Due Diligence Detailed examination of the business affairs of a company, carried out by representatives of a potential purchaser or investor.

Earn out Payments made to vendor which are dependent on targets (set by the purchaser) being met.

Escrow A portion of the purchase consideration held back by the purchaser. It is usually held by lawyers or other agreed third parties, and released contingent on certain conditions being met.

Executive Team A team of individuals chosen to (learn to) run the company completely in your absence.

Exit Leaving the company, often by selling your shares.

Exit timetable The time taken to develop the company to be ready for the actual exit.

Exit strategy A plan devised to enable one to leave the company by selling it, or by some other means.

Factoring Schemes offered by companies to buy from you the debt outstanding from your customers. The factoring company then chases up the debt.

FIFO (First in, First out) This is a method of calculation of stock values. The oldest costs are charged out, the remaining stock is valued at the most recent price.

Guarantees Statements declaring that there are no unfortunate or unstated, unsound or flawed situations or facts that will arise in the future. Guarantees carry full retrospective responsibility.

Guarantor liability Shareholders or partners who assign a lease give guarantees that they will make restitution if the new lessee defaults on payment or terms.

Goodwill A term used in accounting, representing assets within a company that have no tangible value.

Gross profit The difference between 'buy in' price and 'sell out' price often referred to as 'contribution'.

IOD Institute of Directors.

IT Information technology (your computing system).

Investment company A company which makes its living by investing in other companies, often for a share of equity.

LIFO (Last in, First out) A method of calculation of stock values.

Loan stock Loans made to the company but secured on specific assets of the company (excluding shares).

Management accounts Accounts prepared on a frequent (often monthly) basis, used by the management to monitor company progress.

Market potential Opportunities that exist, and are not yet exploited, to sell and supply a company's products/services. This is especially interesting where it can be shown that there are new markets, as yet not approached.

MBI (Management Buy In) A group of people buy into and run a business themselves. Generally a lot of money will need to be raised from external sources to do this.

MBO (Management Buy Out) Existing management within a company buy the whole or part of the company to run themselves. Usually external sources will finance this scheme.

Net profit Profit of the company having deducted all supply and running costs. This is often stated as being 'before tax', or 'after tax'.

Non-executive directors Sometimes referred to as 'independent directors'. Members of the board of directors who do not have an appointed managerial post. They often have jobs in other companies. Their role is to make available their experience, expertise, and bring balance to a board.

NPAT Notional profit after taxation.

P/E ratio Price earning ratio. This is an accounting term which divides the earnings per share into the market price of the share. However, it is often used as an indication of how a company is viewed by investors. A high number PE/ratio denotes an attractive company with potential, whereas a low PE/ratio indicates a company with less attractive prospects. The PE/ratio is used in the calculation of a company's market valuation.

Preference shares A share which entitles the holder to a fixed percentage dividend, often ahead of 'ordinary' shareholders.

Sale proceeds The amount received by the shareholders upon selling the business.

Second tier sale This describes the sale of property or intellectual assets as a secondary activity to the main sale.

SME Small and medium size enterprise. This denotes the size of a business, from small one-man bands, through to medium size in turnover, privately owned and not quoted on the Stock Exchange.

Supply chain This covers procurement of **all** goods, whether raw materials, overhead services, or ancillary products and services.

Supply chain management This covers the process of procurement from sourcing suppliers and products, through negotiating terms of business, cost reduction achievement, communications and administration management, delivery and quality control.

TUPE (Transfer of Undertakings (Protection of Employment)) This is a government regulation introduced to safeguard employees where businesses change owners, or there are changes in service contracting. The latest information and methods of compliance will be known by legal advisers and can also be viewed on the internet.

Venture capital (funds) Money to finance projects usually provided in exchange for some equity within the company borrowing the funds. The lender will generally be a member of the British Venture Capital Association.

Warranties Statements and assurances given by the vendor that can be relied upon.

Index